T0356402

BLOWING UP
EVERYTHING
IS BEAUTIFUL

BLOWING UP EVERYTHING IS BEAUTIFUL

ISRAEL'S EXTERMINATION OF GAZA

JAMES ROBINS

Arcade Publishing • New York

Arcade Publishing books may be purchased in bulk at special discounts for sales promotion, corporate gifts, fund-raising, or educational purposes. Special editions can also be created to specifications. For details, contact the Special Sales Department, Arcade Publishing, 307 West 36th Street, 11th Floor, New York, NY 10018 or info@skyhorsepublishing.com.

Arcade Publishing® is a registered trademark of Skyhorse Publishing, Inc.®, a Delaware corporation.

Visit our website at www.skyhorsepublishing.com.

10 9 8 7 6 5 4 3 2 1

Library of Congress Cataloging-in-Publication Data is available on file.

Print ISBN: 978-1-6482-1155-3
eBook ISBN: 978-1-6482-1156-0

Jacket design by David Ter-Avanesyan
Cover photo by Getty Images

Printed in the United States of America

CONTENTS

now there is a monstrous map that is called Nowhere
and that is where we're all headed, behind it
there is a view called the Province of Mercy,
where the only government is that of the apples
and the only army the wide banners of barley
and its farms are simple, and that is the vision
that narrows in the irises of the dying
and the tired whom we leave in ditches
before they stiffen and their brows go cold
as the stones that have broken our shoes,
as the clouds that grow ashen so quickly after dawn
over palm and poplar, in the deceitful sunrise
of this, your new century.

—Derek Walcott, *The Prodigal*

Whoever stays
until the end
will tell the story

**—Dr. Abu Nujaila, Al-Awda Hospital
October 20, 2023**

WHILE LOOKING
HEAVEN IN THE EYE

February 2025

The war is not over.

Don't lie to yourself. The war is only suspended. Stasis reigns. Gaza is now the place where the most child amputees live. The razing is so complete you can glimpse the Mediterranean from central Rafah. Are those Zaher's hands under the crossbeam? Are those Feeda's bones? Is that Mostafa's head? "Don't be impressed by the forced joy of our enemy," says Bezalel Smotrich. "This is an animalistic society that sanctifies death. Very soon, we will erase their smile again and replace it with cries of grief and the wails of those who were left with nothing."[1] The bombers still hurtle over the town of Jabalia, briefly forbidden to release their deadly freight. Soldiers shuffle back to a perimeter seven hundred meters inside the border fence and prepare to go again. Artillery crews tend their weapons behind sandbag emplacements, enjoying hot meals and better latrines. For the targeting officer, the intelligence man, here is a prized chance to stretch his legs, maybe see his girlfriend; in basements and prefabs, in the Negev desert facility where endless server-banks thrum in the night, his computer still blinks and runs its tallies: faces and names of a surviving multitude; selecting, collating, weighting the figures, slating them all for future end.

The war is not over. Don't lie to others. We have only reached another intermission. Every faceless, paneless window from Remal to Nuseirat was once the prism by which you could look upon a regular Gazan family and find nothing more remarkable than their own way of being in the world, their habits and loves and quiddity. *Zibdiyit Gambari*—a furiously spicy prawn tagine—on a Thursday night. Shisha on the corniche. A moment's breath in Jundi park. Leila Khaled's face proud on the wall of Al-Azhar's campus. Only in their absence do we find a difference: that they were murdered so easily. There are, and will be still, families who do not make the voyage back. Even if their house still stands, the apartment block cratered but upright, even if the neighbors arrive to find that white flag still draped across several balconies and mockingly littered with bullet holes, there will be some places that see no returnees, no survivors at all. The Mughrabi family: 70 killed in a single airstrike. The Abu al-Qumssans: 80 dead by spring. The Salem clan: 270 of them, vanished from the earth. The war has made entire bloodlines extinct.[2]

The war lives. Do not trust in the optimism of butchers, for they itch to unsheathe their cleavers. January 27—a Monday—saw the checkpoints on the coast road at

Netzarim lifted. The north of Gaza, long blockaded, was open again. It took eleven hours for the rivulet of humanity to cover the nine-mile journey, making their way back to the only place they'd ever known as home. Malak Tantesh, a correspondent for *The Guardian*, found nothing of her old life in Beit Lahia:

> We decided to visit our own home for the first time since the war started. I grew up in this area but it had been so devastated, buildings and streets and gardens bombed and demolished, that we could no longer find our way to the house. We were wandering lost and confused, when a neighbour appeared and guided us. The only things still standing were the trunks of a walnut tree, and some olive trees that used to be in our yard. Seeing them there, surrounded only by rubble, I felt like I had been stabbed in my heart. Our home was a three-storey building, and the levels had collapsed on top of each other like layers in a cake. I walked around and over the ruins to see if there was a way in, to recover anything from our life. It was dangerous but our memories deserve it. I couldn't find even the smallest hole. Nothing had survived. My memories, my family's memories and everything we owned have all been crushed and buried.[3]

What is left up here in the churn of a modern no-man's-land? The unnamed, uncounted, unburied dead. And their smell. In preparation for the Nuremberg tribunals in 1945, the Allies sprayed disinfectant over the mash of the city they flattened. It was to mask the putrefaction, so that justice might be tried.[4] Who shall provide the bleach for Gaza? Who will try justice for them? Gaza's Health Ministry, run by Hamas's civilian wing, counts the dead. Their lists have always been reliable, even if they blend the names of fighters with noncombatants.[5] They do not count the missing. The only way to count the missing is to now dig their bones from under grit and gravel. Infection without medicine will claim more. Pneumonia for the elderly out in the open. Malarial water pooled in shell holes. Is it possible to die of a broken heart? Gaza knows. The toll rises, without bombs. This is how the war lives on.

No future, says the war. Do not dream of anything but dust, blast pressure, and want. Don't forget how hungry you were, under that tent flap. What has been done can be done again. What has been done *will* be done again. The bombs are held in suspension, like inverted zeppelins, in the air above. They blot all sunlight. They are coming. You can smell the rivets, the Tritonal. They are always coming. The war lives so long as the debt it incurs lives on the ledger. Carnage costs. The population of several countries will spend decades paying back piecemeal what was remitted for the murder of another all at once. From the United States alone: *$17.9 billion in cash and ammunition.*[6] The war endures, grinds on, consumes more—less noisy than it was before but still present, still imminent, devouring worth and meaning, sanity and dignity, pride and shelter. Between 5 and 10 percent of all munitions dropped, the UN estimates, failed to detonate.[7] Gaza is a graveyard. It is also a minefield.

The war thrives in the memory. Not *remembrance*: the deadweight of an ancient crypt, an elegant mausoleum, a memorial to the fallen lead-cast on its catafalque, the places pilgrims go in dwindling numbers down the years. Such things—these icons—come later, when the war is truly over. No, the war thrives in the mind. It has a vivid, livid life there. It blends flashback and echo with reality. It lashes and curdles everyday life—as much as this life can be called everyday. Night terrors and bed-wetting. Abrupt tantrums, futile rages, surprised tears at a cracked kitchen sink. It makes as its product long months of malaise and weakness, kneads like dough a depression immune to balm. The war strikes again when, having moved the bricks of a collapsed wall all day, you can move bricks no longer. The war puts you on alert, hardwired in that animal part of the brain prone to flinch. A car backfiring could be another knock on the roof. A sweet-seller's reciting of prices sounds, at a distance, like a Merkava tank's loudspeaker. The boys' argument over football downstairs sounds similar to that woman's fight with her husband about whether to stay put or leave south. The war is in the betrayed happiness of reaching for the hand of a friend only to find it gone. And in the look of a quiet grandparent who has seen this all before and fears he doesn't want to live to see it again.

Mahmoud is a taxi driver from Gaza City. One day after the ceasefire, he carried the body of his eleven-year-old daughter to a cemetery. "She was like a bird, so light in my arms," he told the journalist Mohammed Mhawish:

I couldn't find a burial shroud, so I wrapped her in her favorite pink blanket and walked to the cemetery. No car, no ambulance. Just me and her. I kept whispering, "Don't be scared, *habibti*. Baba's here." I remember the mornings when I would drive her to school. The road feels so empty now.

Mhawish spoke to a thirty-four-year-old nurse named Nadia, who for ten days held vigil by an empty crib, whispering a lullaby:

I still hum to her like I used to when she was here. Every night, I rock the cradle and close my eyes, and pretend she's still here. Sometimes I wake up and reach for her, then I feel the bed is empty. This silence is the loudest sound I've ever heard.[8]

Over Gaza hangs the eye: the immense machine of surveillance and collection so sensitive that a woman cannot sneeze in Zeitoun without the Israelis worrying it might be a rocket launch. It used to be wiretaps, letter-opening; now it is a digital dragnet scraping the Strip, upturning all secrets. What does the eye see, this penetrating panoptic eye? The war's leavings and detritus, fury churned in its gusts. Rebar lattice, concrete mulch, fat dogs nuzzling the slabs. The eye records all, electronic as well as flesh, and passes it on to the gunners. Unit 8200 will watch the gang of workers begin to dig around the place someone was last seen, just as it watched the mattresses bundled and borne on backs go down Salah al Din Road in an endless column, just as it has seen the arm of a young software engineer trying to reach out but held back by its cannula, against a field of hungry flame. What do we see of the eye? Our view, looking back, is glaucous, super-occluded, disguised by classification. *Sodi Beyoter*, Top Secret. You are not supposed to know what the eye sees; you are not allowed to know. For we are still in a time of war, and war demands as its penultimate tribute the words out of your mouth and the knowledge from your ears.

The war is not over. That is why the eye persists, never blinks. The war goes on because the Occupation goes on. It is in the nature of occupations that they should lead, with the certainty of the seasons, to Pyrrhic bouts of bloodletting. Until the fact of the Occupation joins the cut strands of history, only truces can be called and ceasefires agreed. It is the font from which all of this horror flows. Dam it up, seal the torrent at its mouth, or the war goes on forever.

* * *

The journalism collected here is a record, in real time, of a cataclysm.

For fifteen months Israel's army, air force, and intelligence corps, under order of the state's political leaders and lawyers, in close alliance with the settler movement, made it clear that Palestinian life was undesirable. Beneath the mask of a war against the militant party Hamas, there was a campaign of punishment against the people of Gaza for the offense of existing. War is the zone where will meets possibility. This war's purpose and principal aim was to obliterate the possibility of survival.

This war—this cataclysm—did not begin modestly with noble aims and pure hearts, only later afflicted by the debauch and cruelty which wars by their nature breed. Born innocent, touched lightly by the charge of mass murder, of extermination? No, murder was massive from the first day, obscene from the first hour. The methods of destruction were elaborate, determined, and total.[9] In aid of traditional military means—bombardment from air and land; incursions, raids, and massacres; the holding of territory—was a series of actions whose victims *could only be civilians.* Gaza's regular prewar blockade was tightened so as to stifle the necessities of life until an entire society choked. Food, water, fuel, medicine: all cut off, as well as any chance of escape. Since 1967 Israel has held the power of life and death over Gaza and its people, and since October 2023, it chose death instead of life. Accessory campaigns complete the picture. Pinpoint targeting of the press *as a group*, to curtail the truth. Calculated attacks on relief workers *as a group*, to slow the sharing of aid. A schema of cultural destruction to wither this land's distinct history and damage its many faiths. For those the Israeli army could not kill, an answer was also found: the specific and elaborate wreckage of clinics, aid stations, humanitarian convoys, and hospitals.

To feed and stoke the taking of life, Israel's political class made it clear to the riflemen and pilots and tankers under their command—as they made it clear to all of Israeli society, and the world—that Palestinians were less than human, deserving of death, and worthy of comparison to the Jews' worst biblical enemies, or to the Nazis. Wars also do well at elevating the generals into ranks of authority well above politicians. In a state as heavily militarized as Israel, this blending of the uniformed and the elected took place long ago. And the politicians were more forceful, clear-eyed, and vengeful than the troops at their command, sparing no shame in saying exactly what they wished to happen, and how brutally. *They told you what they were doing while they did it.* Compiled here is a record of what was done—the first history of the attempt to annihilate Gaza.

This book has an argument to make, a case to prosecute, and it has its enemies. These enemies should be enemies of us all, as they have made themselves true enemies of humanity. Not just on the simple basis that murder is a wicked thing that invokes and begs for punishment. The argument is made on a more radical basis: murderers operate in a system which enables their crime and makes it easier to inflict, then later eases their consciences. Meanwhile, the system coats our understanding of that crime in a pall of mystification, propaganda, and lies. Do not look away. Place your fist on the scale. Otherwise, this system, as its last redeeming act and as it was designed to do, will work tirelessly for the exoneration of the murderer.

Neither do these essays find meaning and worth in false modesty. They do not stoop to even-handedness, or seek consolations for the reader in fictions, be they legal, political, or moral. For these fictions have been as readily ruined as Palestinian homes, bakeries, colleges, limbs, and sanity. I make these charges precisely so the perpetrator might, if even at a distance and at an oblique angle, feel some sting of the reality of their grim work—certainly more than they might feel in their own land, which nurses these crimes over and over again, then covers them in soil.

* * *

Breaching the walls that held them captive on the morning of October 7, 2023, Hamas's militants did not drive from Gaza into their occupier's territory to find a serene nation at peace with itself.

Israeli society was convulsing. Since January of that year, Prime Minister Benjamin Netanyahu's Likud-led government had been trying to wreck the country's legal system by removing the power of the Supreme Court to overturn unconstitutional laws. It was an early warning. An augur of what was to come. Netanyahu was showing the world exactly how much respect he had for any limit on his power, any shackle on the state. Yet in return, and with outrage, Israelis were putting up a fight. A vast and principled opposition formed, and the nation split: between those who wanted to save the last fragments of democracy and secularism still protected by the country's Basic Laws, and those who wanted the government to fully embrace authoritarianism at home to go with the authoritarianism it inflicted on its inland empire.

A single crystalline thread joined together Netanyahu's trial on corruption charges, his "judicial reform" project, and the later transformation of Gaza into a province where nearly every code and clause of international law—let alone Israel's own—could be violated. The violence and vandalism necessary to retain Israel's place as overlord in the territories ricocheted back to afflict the society from which it came.[10] Saul Friedländer, ninety-one years old, an escapee from the Shoah, and Israel's most eminent scholar on that subject, feared the worst. "The vibrant country I lived and worked in for decades is dead," he wrote trembling to his diary. "Something else, something unacceptable, has taken its place."[11]

Other than the paratroopers, the most revered soldiers in the Israeli military are its pilots. Few are as important to Israel's idealized self-image as they, and none more vital to its overwhelming firepower. The political crisis in 2023 grew so fractious than even reservist airmen threatened to mutiny if Netanyahu's judicial reform was passed. The IDF, as a conscript force, reflects and heightens the divisions of its society. Including in its intelligence department, where dysfunction that year proved lethal. Unit 8200, the most elite and secretive spy operation, possessed detailed plans of Hamas's rampage on October 7—a forty-page-long document called "Jericho Wall"—and yet no commander heeded the alerts.[12] "Will an attack from the outside save the Jewish state before internal turmoil destroys it?" Friedländer worried.[13] He soon had his answer. Holes were blown in the fence the spies were supposed to be guarding—achieving what the Great March of Return in 2018 could not—and Hamas's brigades fanned out across the sand.

Like the war it provoked, the militants' assault that day was part-counterforce, part-pogrom. Checkpoints were trashed, barracks set on fire, and police stations blasted. Roughly one third of the casualties were troops or cops. Another third were partiers at the Nova music festival—a very literal definition of a killing field. And there were the *kibbutz:* Be'eri and Nahal Oz, among others, their floors smeared in blood, their children plucked from communal life into captivity.

In the same way the Palestinian resistance might've enjoyed greater popular support if it had only attacked military targets, so Israel might've lived up to its own propaganda if it had embarked on a genuine and serious mission to find those 251 hostages. It might've realized too, as November 2023 and January 2025 proved definitively, that negotiation was the only reliable method for their return.

But humiliation has to be repaid in kind. Vulnerability, weakness, violation: these are intolerable feelings to any culture, most especially those which cherish as the centerpiece of their national myth a sense of invincibility in battle. Palestinians too feel this violation, this weakness—they feel it daily, and without the cathartic advantage of jet bombers. Like the United States after 9/11, a ruthless display of might was the only means to purge this sense of penetration, embarrassment, and grief. What is the point of that might—the fleets of tanks and planes, the enormous network of surveillance, nuclear weapons, the trillions needed to maintain them—if it cannot be wielded? On the evening of October 7, the will to do something with all that annihilating hardware encountered possibility: the possibility of revenge, and the chance to finish its project of conquest between the river and the sea.

> **Isaac Herzog**, Israeli president, October 2023: "It's an entire nation out there that is responsible. It's not true this rhetoric about civilians not aware, not involved. It's absolutely not true . . . and we will fight until we break their backbone."[14]
> **Yoav Gallant**, defense minister, October 2023: "Complete siege on Gaza. No electricity, no food, no water, no fuel. Everything is closed. We are fighting human animals and we are acting accordingly."[15]
> **Itamar Ben-Gvir**, national security minister, November 2023: "When we say that Hamas should be destroyed, it also means those who celebrate, those who support, and those who hand out candy—they're all terrorists, and they should also be destroyed."[16]

Israel Katz, energy minister (later defense minister), October 2023: "All the civilian population in Gaza is ordered to leave immediately. We will win. They will not receive a drop of water or a single battery until they leave the world."[17]

Avi Dichter, agriculture minister, former director of Shin Bet, November 2023: "[We] are now actually rolling out the Gaza Nakba."[18]

Nissim Vaturi, deputy speaker of the Knesset, October 2023, "Now we all have one common goal— to wipe the Gaza Strip off the face of the earth."[19]

Bezalel Smotrich, finance minister, April 2024: "There are no half measures. Rafah, Deir al Balah, Nuseirat—total annihilation. 'You will blot out the remembrance of Amalek from under heaven'—there's no place under heaven."[20]

Amichai Eliyahu, heritage minister, November 2023: "North Gaza is more beautiful than ever. Blowing up and flattening everything is beautiful."[21]

Terror-bombing began immediately. But terror-bombing was regular. Standard operating procedure. "Mowing the grass." This is what the IDF calls the common tactic of paring back the confidence of the militants, shredding a couple hundred Gazans for a few weeks as a deterrent. This was done in 2008, in 2012 and 2014, again in 2021.[22] After October, it would be different. No longer a pruning operation. More like scraping the ground down to its bedrock and salting the remains.[23] The few limits on their behavior vanished— "all restraints," said Yoav Gallant, were removed.[24] The army, like Netanyahu, would not be cuffed by moral sentiment or so weak a thing as the law. A new targeting system was used, made up of three main programs: Lavender, Gospel, and Where's Daddy?. Described as "AI," really these are algorithms to sort and rank targets at a faster rate than any human intelligence officer. Within the International Law Department (an office in the IDF's Military Advocate General's Corps), a deadly ratio was established: fifteen to twenty civilians could be killed for even the lowest-ranking *suspected* militant. The ratio was so extreme it obliterated the principle of "proportionality." Israeli gunners behaved as though it didn't exist at all.

The geography of Gaza is not hard to understand. A near-rectangular block of land, laced down its spine north to south by a chain of cities tracing the Mediterranean coast: Gaza City, the largest urban area, near the top; Deir al Balah followed by Khan Younis; Rafah at the bottom. It was in this direction that the greater mass of Palestinians alive in the Strip—around two million—were forced to flee by the IDF. And while they fled, waves of mutilation rained on them. In those first feverish months, an average of 350 Palestinians were murdered every day in airstrikes. Almost half of the 29,000 munitions dropped by the Israeli air force were unguided, imprecise "dumb bombs."[25]

December 1, 2023, was the day a method began to combine with madness. Already 90 percent of Gaza's population was "displaced"—the UN's euphemism for being torn from your home, made a refugee in your own land, and lacking anywhere to go that could be considered more safe than anywhere else. Not the hospitals: 14,000 people were sheltering near al-Quds hospital in western Gaza City when it was repeatedly bombed in late October. Not the churches: the Greek Orthodox Saint Porphyrius, said to be the third oldest of its kind in the world, was struck as five hundred people cowered under its eaves. On the first day of December, the IDF debuted a map vivisecting the Strip into 620 parcels and sectors. Suburb by suburb, street by street. Enclaves, exclaves, carve-outs, "safe zones." The next phase would be calculated. Cell phone reception and internet access were cut; word of mouth and the leaflets the IDF dropped from the sky were the only reliable way for Gazans to be told where to find a haven. But even the designated "humanitarian areas" were not exempt from the terror-bombing. Then the ground troops rolled in. No place in Gaza would be left untouched by these raids, incursions, and airstrikes—these occupations within the Occupation.

With the infantry came new dangers. The IDF's common practice was to designate the area around a unit's position as a "combat zone." The better term might be "free-fire zone." There was no signage posted at the boundaries, and no warnings given at the outer limit. Anyone straying into these areas was shot on sight. If they were men, their corpses were counted as "terrorists." The longer Israeli troops occupied Gaza, the more the chain of command seemed to break down. Or did it? Looting was also common practice: grunts filming themselves in wrecked living rooms, eating Palestinian food, raiding cash from under mattresses, spraying graffiti on the walls, then dynamiting the entire block. Surgeons and medics unanimously reported that among the countless blast and crush wounds were victims, often children, killed by a single large-caliber bullet: evidence of sharpshooters. Repeated raids on al-Shifa and Nasser hospitals left shallow mass graves in their wake, hundreds of bodies. One perverse genre of memento—which IDF troops were not shy of posting online—saw them rifling through wardrobes for women's underwear. In one photograph, a private dangles a pair of white briefs over the open mouth of a comrade pretending to sleep. Another gormless mouth-open snap shows a soldier cupping the plastic breasts of a bare mannequin. Tongue lolling like a frat animal, one trooper pretends to pinch the nipple of another soldier wearing a bra too small for him.[26]

Each of the 620 parcels of divided land was transformed into its own miniature terra nullius. Any behavior, no matter how vulgar or how criminal, was allowed. In May, in the Zeitoun neighborhood of Gaza City, soldiers of the Nahal Brigade discovered an elderly couple in their home, too old and infirm to flee. The troops took the eighty-year-old man, tied an explosive fuse around his neck then ordered him, hobbling on his cane, to clear houses for eight hours. They let their human shield go at the end of his forced labor, but didn't inform the surrounding units. The couple made it a hundred meters down the road before another brigade shot them both.[27] Did the army really go rogue? No, the soldiers were fulfilling the deeper mission laid out for them by their commanders—both civil and military. Their president said there were no uninvolved civilians, and this, in turn, became the army's motto. They behaved exactly as they were instructed.

In defense of their ability to act however they liked, Israel mustered its allies: Germany, Britain, and above all, the United States. Each lie told, every excuse offered by politicians, every rationale crafted by their mouthpieces was to protect a war being made on the most helpless. In the first six months of the war, 44 percent of all victims were children. *Yes, yes, we deeply regret all these casualties*, the allies sighed, *we wish that it weren't necessary.* You could hear how earnest they were, that particular tone of voice used before the inevitable "but" comes along. To what crime would you make yourself an accessory? To what atrocity will you make yourself an accomplice? The answer given by countless powerful people, standing before the judgment of the world looking upon the image of the body parts of a child smearing the inside of a dirty plastic bag, was to say *Yes, here is a worthy thing; long may it continue.* But such a defense was never made on principle, and certainly not a principle that could be laid both ways as the journalist Tom Stevenson did:

> One might wonder what the response would be if the arguments deemed good enough to justify the attack on Gaza were inverted. Suppose national newspapers were to argue that because the government of Israel has ordered hideous atrocities, as it certainly has, Israeli officials should be killed at any cost, and if Tel Aviv must be destroyed to achieve this then so be it. If the bars of Rehavia must be turned into rubble, too bad—besides, look how close they are to the presidency on HaNasi Street. Has the Israeli state "diverted funds" to the building of underground bunkers for its leadership? Is carpet bombing justified on the grounds that the government and the political parties that constitute it are "integrated into

Israeli society"? Arguments as absurd as these acquire
respectability in the service of killing Palestinians.[28]

Israel has long counted the calories entering Gaza. Even
in peacetime the land is not large enough to support the
people who live there encaged.[29] Within weeks, and with
a total siege imposed upon them, the threat of famine
quickly appeared. The nature of the siege—so easily laid on
an already captive population—also kept its infrastructure
in a middling state. Knocking out sanitation plants and
treatment facilities quickly turned the Strip's water supply
to a dribble. What water that could be found was already
infested with typhus and cholera. Farmers, had they dared
to tend their small plots, would've been shot near the border
wall. And so one part of a nation was made to eat the rice
that made it through the gauntlet from the outside world.
When even that was restricted, one part of a nation ate
animal feed, weeds, and hay. Starvation. Hunger. Famine.
These too were the weapons at Israel's hand.[30] The world has
not seen urban hunger this extreme and concentrated since
the siege of Leningrad ended in 1944.[31]

That any aid was let in at all was a great sin in the eyes
of one group. The illegal occupation and colonization of
Palestinian lands—the tax breaks and subsidies to encourage them, the military needed to defend them—had produced a faction in Israeli society that is somehow both *of* the
state yet in permanent rebellion against it; a political movement violently opposed to the state's secular form even as it
hopes to enlarge that state's territory. Israel's Id: the settlers.

Elections in late 2022 saw the settlers' most virulent—
let us say it openly: fascist—figureheads enter government

alongside the Likud: Otzma Yehudit (Jewish Power, led by Itamar Ben-Gvir) and HaTzionut HaDatit (Religious Zionism, led by Bezalel Smotrich). While the settlers' domain had only expanded in the West Bank since Netanyahu's first term as prime minister, they had been defeated in Gaza—their crass subdivisions dismantled in 2005 during the "Disengagement Plan." They wanted, and still want, a *reconquista*. And in this goal, they saw what the Israeli government was doing with clearer eyes than anyone else in the country, or in the West. While the Israeli government and its backers officially denied killing civilians, the settlers saw that they were, and believed it was good. The bloodletting of Palestinians, the demolitions, the bombings: the settlers cheered it all on in the belief that it was to purify their desired real estate of any opposition. The movement did its part too: appearing daily at the border crossings to block the passage of aid trucks. Often, these settler mobs were tipped off by local police when the shipments were coming through.[32] It was from this coalition—as well as the Likud-linked think tanks and intelligence departments in Tel Aviv—that plans emerged aiming at the total resettlement of the Gazan population outside Gaza. To Sinai, maybe; to other Arab countries; to vapors on the wind. They called it "voluntary," of course. Yet as Shlomo Karhi, the communications minister, made clear at the settlers' jubilant conference in January 2024, voluntary is "a state you impose [on someone] until they give their consent."

By May 2024, three-quarters of the entire population of Gaza were crammed into the sector around the southernmost city of Rafah. Having chased them there, the IDF sought to chase them out again, though not before thinning their numbers. Even US president Joe Biden—or at least those palace guards around him, the fanatical circle who made policy on his behalf—threatened to withhold precious munitions should an invasion of Rafah go ahead.[33] Biden had an advantage he could've wielded, if he was of a mind to do so: a provisional order issued by the International Court of Justice to immediately cease all military operations in Rafah. Of course, as with all American advice and mock admonition, it was easier to withdraw the threat than issue it in the first place. When the IDF took control over the border crossing into Egypt, the siege first announced in October was finally complete. To celebrate, they drove a tank over the small sign at its entrance that read "I Love Gaza."[34] Some 600,000 people fled out of Rafah, back to the squalid mess made of Deir al Balah and Khan Younis.

An undulating tide of brokenness stretching to the horizon, from border wall to sea, and back in history to Hanoi, to Dresden, to Guernica. To look upon the miserable vista made of Gaza is to think of the bombers above. Why else did arms shipments contain so many Mark 82 munitions, 500 pounds in weight with a lethal area of 25,000 square feet? Or the Mark 84, three times as heavy with a deadly radius of 500,000 square feet? But the wastes were also made more intimately. By tank shells and artillery, above all by demolition teams. Like the photographs of troopers in looted panties, the genre of "controlled demolition selfie" became ubiquitous: cheers as the blasting caps go off, some school, some university, an entire city block coming down. By January 2025, IDF engineers were running low on plastic explosive. Nearly 70 percent of all buildings in Gaza are either damaged or destroyed completely. A full 92 percent of those are homes.[35] This land, more so than it ever was before, is a camp of concentration fit only for the habitation of rats and dogs. Vines wither. The land dries fallow. By December—enduring a full year of immiseration—a survey revealed a mood in Gaza that should have made, if we lived in a just world, the blood of every soul within it run cold. Of the Palestinian children still surviving in Gaza, 96 percent felt their death was imminent. Of the Palestinian children in Gaza, 46 percent said they would rather die than continue living.[36]

After harrying these survivors down the length of Gaza for nearly a year, blasting them as they fled, Israel returned to where the war had begun: the north, only with a new tactic—a tactic inconceivably more pitiless than anything tried yet. The Generals' Plan was composed by a clutch of retired officers led by Giora Eiland. It was never formally adopted. At least the Israeli security cabinet insisted it wasn't. However, from October 2024 until January 2025, the Generals' Plan is precisely what was inflicted on everything above Gaza City: a siege-within-a-siege laid against the towns of Beit Hanoun, Beit Lahia, and the Jabalia refugee camp. Instead of calling in settler gangs to obstruct the passage of aid, the army itself cut all humanitarian supplies themselves, then maneuvered to close the noose. Eiland's plan said civilians should be given a week to flee. They were given mere hours. Anyone left inside this zone, Eiland insisted, was by definition a terrorist. But, by this point, what did it matter? The Israeli government and its army had long since given up the fiction of "combatants" and "innocents."

At the point of its most acute brutality—a brutality that strained belief even from its *first* day—the war ceased. Except it did not cease. It was paused, stopped at the checkpoint, sent back to the waiting room. The terms of the truce agreed in mid-January 2025 were no different than what had been offered in May 2024. Biden admitted it, was proud of it.[37] And so from May until January a further 12,000 lives were thrown away—60 percent of whom were children, women, and the elderly—for no goal, no gain, and no other reason than Benjamin Netanyahu's vanity and to save Joe Biden's face.

* * *

Like the Netzarim Corridor cleaving Gaza in halves, our era has been split surgically in two. On one side: all the illusions and myths we pulled tight to us in comfort. On the other side: the starkness of fact, and the facts of blood. There is Before Gaza, where we once lived. And there is After Gaza, our new home.

To the beforetime belongs everything we once told ourselves about human wickedness. That it could be contained and prevented. That it might be outlawed by instruments of noble and genius design. If human action was capable of terrible things, perhaps marvelous things too were in its grasp. Great plans were laid after World War I, brave ideas to prevent naked power from scouring the earth. It did not work. A project stillborn.[38] Only after World War II did these plans find a moment to match their aspiration. We believed in its ideals: of tolerance, the long slow stamping out of prejudice, equal protection for all, anywhere. Never Again was its slogan, written on the mountainsides and plains of history with charnel ash collected from Auschwitz. Those words were supposed to be immovable. Eternal. With this faith, this optimism, rising out of the midnight of the century, we strengthened the codes to prevent atrocity. Even if those codes failed, perhaps those people who made the atrocity might be punished, their humbling made into a deterrence for the future.

What shall we call this belief, these codes? Call it The Moral Order of the World.

In the beforetime, the story we wanted to tell ourselves—the story of inching human progress and the conquering of our own worst habits—was as vital as the law we invented and the politics to complement them. Its first chapter, written in wide italics, was the Judgment at Nuremberg, when the victorious Allies self-consciously distanced themselves from old ways of doing things. There would be imperial carve-ups and occupations and a flood of expelled peoples, yes, but these acts were the price paid to create a new regime: a universal regime of principle and law. And anyway, the Allies said, even if there were a few breaches here and there, the *aspiration* to do better is what mattered most. The Judeocide of 1933 to 1945 was one thread in this new regime's canvas, but it was not the whole picture. Rules were fashioned from scratch, in the face of the cries of conservatives who wanted sovereignty and legal precedent to be the outermost bounds of reform. Crimes of aggression were outlawed. Something called "crimes against humanity" was defined and prohibited. The United Nations was conjured, and one of its first acts of business was to enthrone a convention against genocide. To hear that charge, the International Court of Justice was resurrected.

A long interlude followed, to allow for the Cold War. A first sign, perhaps, that these beliefs—these *aspirations*—did not clad states or governments in fresh iron. The rules could be bent. And so atrocities continued. The middle decades of the twentieth century brim with them, and with bones. In Cambodia and Indonesia, in Bangladesh and Chile, in Biafra and Palestine, atrocity revealed the flaw in the manufacture of the new regime. There were many crimes, it turned out, a state or a party could commit without rousing the law. To duck under the bar of criminality, a government could wield the same tools used by the Allied powers immediately after 1945: carve-ups, occupations, resettlements. Military operations were a convenient cover behind which crimes against civilians could be hidden. Even aggressive warfare, defined at Nuremberg as the premier sin, could be excused and forgiven, as in Vietnam. Because most states wanted to reserve these prerogatives for themselves, they failed to denounce them in others. In the cauldron of the Cold War, the Moral Order of the World revealed cracks and dents in its own foundation. Some were built into the order by design; others were made to spite it.

In these years the Moral Order of the World faced what looked like its most severe challenge. A peace movement— principled, radical, global—said over and over again that no regime claiming to be moral could ever coexist with nuclear weapons. They thrust a finger at the suppurating waste left of Vietnam and said *You are making another Holocaust*, then threatened to tear down the American government when it refused to listen. Perhaps the rules were not the problem, one part of the peace movement charged. Perhaps they worked perfectly fine, serving their role in defending a system that needed domination to fuel itself. Other parts of the peace movement looked to the spoliation of the natural world and suggested a new crime: ecocide. If only we'd listened, back then.

These were years of weakness. But the beforetime was not yet spent. The Moral Order of the World had a while left to run. In fact, it grew stronger. The moment of unchallenged American dominance was also the moment of the Moral Order's most expansive flourishing. The struggle against atrocity and mass murder breathed anew. Vast fields of scholarship were conjured. Old militarism was dressed in the fresh rags of "humanitarian intervention." Universal jurisdiction entered the lexicon of law, and with it the International Criminal Court. The Shoah emerged as the preeminent evil of our time, the yardstick by which all other crimes were measured. Intellectuals spoke of this new empire of freedom without fear of hypocrisy. This was a paradox, surely? The dominion of human rights and international law was built by cooperation, tolerance, negotiation; it depended on the consent of every signatory, and asserted by virtue its principles into being. It couldn't be imposed from on high by one state alone, because that would be something else, a different order entirely. Could it be that the Moral Order was something the hegemon gets to wear like a gold-plated sidearm? They alone decide when it shall be drawn, when fired. Among the elites who considered themselves guardians of the Moral Order, there was a regnant belief that the War on Terror was a *fulfillment* of its promises rather than another sustained offensive against it. This war against a feeling—still ongoing, for no war on an emotion can ever truly be won—revealed where the threat really came from. It was not the peace movement, not any-more. It wasn't even the jihadis. The Moral Order of the World was crippled by its own author.

"How did you go bankrupt?" asks one character in Hemingway's *The Sun Also Rises*. "Two ways," comes the reply. "Gradually and then suddenly."[39]

We have entered the future now, seen its bruised eyes. We have entered the aftertime, touched its quivering flesh. Humanity's achievement is perhaps a mountain—but a mountain of platitudes.[40]

If we were to be quite serious with ourselves, no con-science should be asked to keep its balance in a world where death on Gaza's scale is possible. And so, like peace move-ments past, and as it has done so many times before, the con-science of humanity made its appeal to the powerful. Who were they, this unified, undaunted, outraged conscience? The UN agencies and aid groups. The volunteer doctors, the lawyers. Journalists, diplomats, academics. Dedicated activists, veteran and virgin. The students. The Palestinian diaspora, antizionist Jews. Larger in number than all of them combined: the greater mass of the people, who did not have access or lanyards, or a garland of credentials after their name but who, with enough empathy, could imagine themselves and their families in the place of a Palestinian from Shujayya and their family, and decided on this simple basis that what was being done to them was wrong.

For fifteen months the people made their protest. Their pleas were solemn but firm, reinforced by hard evi-dence. Their demonstrations were minimally disruptive. The conscience of humanity—as you might expect—was nonviolent, respectable, and civilized. A few tried tougher

action: in Britain, a small group of militants waged a sabo-
tage operation against arms manufacturers; wearing his Air
Force fatigues, Aaron Bushnell burned himself alive at the
gates of the Israeli embassy in Washington, DC. Still, for
fifteen months, they would not retreat. On their shoulders,
through every city in the West, was carried the name Hind
Rajab. On January 29 2024, this six-year-old girl stayed
on a call with emergency workers for three hours while an
Israeli tank trapped the family car on Gaza City street and
killed six relatives in the car and the two paramedics who
came to rescue her.

"I'm so scared, please come," she said. "Come take me.
Please, will you come?" Then they killed her, too.[41]

In Hind Rajab's name the conscience of humanity did
not ask for new laws, did not insist on wild, too-radical proposals. Instead, their clear demand, repeated with all the
force they could muster, was for the Moral Order of the
World to enforce its existing laws without prejudice, and
to reaffirm the Palestinian right to exist. At the sit-ins and
campus campsites, on the marches and endless open letters,
in legal briefs and magazine essays, they made their sensible
plea for the universal regime of human rights to be applied
universally. In other words: *They did everything right.* They
followed the rules which they had been told were the correct route to reform. With faith in how things are supposed
to work, they aired the facts and invoked the Moral Order's
own standards. And how was the conscience repaid? By
being called anti-Semites, if they were lucky; getting their
heads kicked in by the cops, if they weren't.

Above all, they invoked the most serious word in their
arsenal. Even if "war crimes" or "crimes against humanity"

did not frighten or stir as they should, there was another term that was supposed to trigger overwhelming action, to bring the cavalry over the hill on their behalf. They called it genocide. So totemic a word and accusation, its moral weight drawn from the resonant echo of the Holocaust, was not offered lightly. After Rwanda, after Srebrenica, it should have been enough to make everything stop for a second. Yet in making this charge of genocide, they placed more faith in the Moral Order at precisely the moment when it was revealed to be hollow. When the world needed it most—when the Palestinians of Gaza needed it most—the interlocking system of codes and principles supposed to defend the innocent and helpless could do nothing. Recall the silence that came after the shout: that is the Moral Order of the World speaking back to you. It had nothing to say. "The non-violent oppressed," I. F. Stone once wrote, "cannot twinge the conscience of the oppressor unless he has one."[42]

There was a hope—a hope expressed in some of the reporting collected here—that the case brought against Israel by South Africa at the International Court of Justice, and the arrest warrants issued for Netanyahu and Gallant by the International Criminal Court, might have some propaganda effect beyond the law. Even if the ICJ's provisional measures remain unenforced, and many of the signatories to the Rome Statute collectively decided to dodge their responsibility to deliver fugitives to the ICC, then at least these rulings might strengthen the hand of anyone willing to dissent. It might help the bureaucrats and functionaries—at the State Department on C Street, on the Werderscher Markt in Berlin—to organize a campaign of internal pressure against their own governments. It might provide a legal basis for the revision of the rules which allowed so many guns and so much ammunition to be sent to Israel with such little oversight. It might be the push needed to get hesitant diplomats to begin the work of building international consent for a ceasefire. But this is a consolation. A false hope. Scraps from the table. Either the system functions as we were told it was supposed to, or it doesn't function at all. And it didn't.[43]

Among the litter of history can be found a thousand tales of disillusion, deception, and letdown. Haven't we been here before, conscript and unhappy witnesses to a cataclysm, discovering in the light of a shellburst that the Moral Order of the World was really quite different to what the powerful said it was? Plenty of people have gone through that singular experience which suddenly cracks open all illusions, all myths. Many of us resemble the writer David Rieff arriving in Bosnia in 1994 as it was encircled and besieged by hostile Serbian troops: "If the bad news about Bosnia could just be brought home to people, I remember thinking, the slaughter would not be allowed to continue."[44] But it did continue, then. Just as it continues now. It provokes a bereft feeling, a feeling of being unmoored. It also provokes a forbidding thought—the most forbidding thought. If these people over here can be killed purely because one state wills it, and that killing is made possible by the arms and imprimatur of a superpower, and at the same moment international law is proved powerless, doesn't that mean my own protection is gone? If Palestinian life can be thrown away so easily, mine can too. Aren't I just like them now, alone and undefended? Remember how easily the most powerful nations on earth washed themselves of the stains of a multitude in order to shake the hands of the men who made them corpses. This moment of epiphany is different from the others, for it has never been so starkly revealed and to so many people that they are disposable.

The lessons of the past have not been forgotten so much as deliberately unlearned. The Israeli government is at the blunt pulverizing edge of a global movement that is doing precisely what Yoav Gallant ordered in October: releasing all restraints. Those restraints are universal human rights and international law. In their place, unfettered, is the rule of power for its own end. It was in part for Jewish suffering that the Moral Order of the World was made; it has been finally unmade to protect the Jewish state's brutality. It took eighty years of constant effort to dislodge Never Again from its place. It took one last tempest in Gaza to wipe it away completely. An alliance of primitive instinct, private interest, and technological momentum has triumphed at the expense of humanity and its codes of decency. We proceed into the aftertime, After Gaza. The future has been rehearsed.

A MISSED MORAL LESSON

The Anniversary of October 7

New Republic, **October 2024**

No one should be made to relive that evening, when the smoke was still rising, and the only authority was that of panic. But in the aftermath of October 7, 2023, mingled with the rage, the grief, the humiliation that night, there should have been another feeling: a stunned clarity. That the barbarism and blood visited on the Nova festival and kibbutz Be'eri were mirrors of a blood and barbarism long inflicted on the West Bank and Gaza. That the homelessness of one people was never sound enough reason to enforce homelessness on another. That deterrence and military might will fail if you don't acknowledge why your enemy fights. That the pursuit of domination will never lead to peace or even a tolerable kind of stasis; it leads instead, with depressing regularity, to its gory opposite.

If that day is to have any meaning, if the memory of the dead is to be used for a higher purpose than as license for more murder, it must be in service of a moral lesson: No state can live sanely in a condition of permanent siege. With that lesson, Israel's leaders would have put the planes back in their hangars, reversed the tanks back to their depots, switched off the algorithm that allows them to coolly and clinically slaughter the blameless by the dozen, and on October 8 immediately restarted negotiations for a just peace.

Don't waste time with counterfactuals, we historians are told. Counterfactuals are just fantasies, really, wishful dreams, and they become more deceitful the further they drift from reality. But to mourn the present and wish for something different is not a counterfactual. It is a warning of the kind that has been sounded at every critical juncture of the last eight decades and has always been ignored by those who have the power to behave differently.

The path was laid in 1967, in the euphoria of victory in the Six-Day War and the seizure of what little territory the Palestinians had in their possession. Instead of retreating from what did not belong to it, instead of adhering to the laws and resolutions that told it to withdraw, the Israeli state chose to exalt its armies as colonists of the future. I. F. Stone, as great a moral mind as he was a journalist, saw easily and early what Israel had chosen by refusing peace in favor of a God-given arrogance on the land. Radical though he was, Stone was no Bundist or anti-Zionist. In 1946, he had sailed as a reporter and sympathizer from Poland with survivors and escapees of the Holocaust on what he called the "Jewish Mayflowers," dodging the British blockade to Mandate Palestine. It was worry and fear that made him notice, in 1967, the vise grip tighten:

> The spiral of fear and hate . . . the atmosphere of a besieged community, ringed by hostile neighbours . . . turning every man and woman into a soldier, regarding every Arab within it distrustfully as a potential Fifth Columnist, and glorying in its military strength. Chauvinism and militarism are the inescapable fruits. . . . In the absence of a general settlement, war will recur at regular intervals.[1]

"The finest day," Stone hoped, will be the day Israel "achieves reconciliation," a greater and more permanent triumph than any military victory. Every day since the Six-Day War, and every day since October 7, has been in defiance of these warnings, these hopes. Every day has been proof that generations of leaders could have picked a wiser course and chose not to. Every massacre is a choice.

One of the chief stupidities of the Hamas offensive was to kill, along with many innocents, Israel's reckoning with itself. Since January 2023, the better part of the nation—that part sensitive to the threat of dictatorship—had come out in a monthslong rolling thunder of protest, strike, and civil disobedience against the Likud's "judicial reform," a project of vandalism to strip Israel's Supreme Court of its ability to overturn unconstitutional laws.[2] The so-called reform's twin purposes were to protect Benjamin Netanyahu from seeing prison on corruption charges and to create the opening through which Netanyahu's coalition partners—the Jewish Power and Religious Zionist parties—could intensify their campaign of building new settlements in the West Bank. We regard the word *polarization* with fright and fear of late, but in this case, polarization was necessary and good: The country divided, and those who preferred secular democracy over the whims of hysterical messianists were in the majority.[3]

By October 6, the majority was arriving (slowly and much too late) at a realization that the settler movement incubated in the frontier had returned to infect the very heart of the nation. Even if most could not recognize the need to retreat from that frontier, they noticed what the frontier had done.[4] Made there, on the hilltops of Hebron and Nablus, ringed in wire, in the daily disinterment of someone else's olive groves, was a bacillus of fanaticism and bloodlust. Israel had not annexed the territories; the territories had annexed Israel. So it was that during Passover in 2023, a squad of the faithful (partly incited by Itamar Ben-Gvir) tried to get to the Temple Mount in Jerusalem to perform a ritual sacrifice.[5] In return, Palestinian youths tried to fortify the Al Aqsa mosque against them, only to be cleared out roughly by Israeli police.[6] Thus October 7 earned its grotesque name, Al Aqsa Flood; thus Stone Age rituals provoked Stone Age justice; thus Israeli citizens were denied a showdown with Netanyahu's settler coalition, the chance to finally excise them from political life.

A misguided strain of liberal thinking places blame for the disaster of October 7 and all subsequent disasters on Benjamin Netanyahu alone. Profoundly corrupt, decisively incompetent, savage to his toes, only he could have made the Jewish state the least safe place on earth for Jews.[7] With any luck, the rest of Netanyahu's life will be spent in a small prison cell—whether in The Hague or in Tel Aviv. He knows this, so the deeper and wider he makes the war on Gaza, and now on Lebanon, the longer he will put off the inevitable. This is why, the argument goes, he has personally sabotaged every proposal for a ceasefire, no matter how reasonable, no matter how necessary for the rescue of the hostages he claims to care about so much.[8]

However, if we were honest with ourselves, the ugliness of this picture would not meaningfully ease with Netanyahu removed from the frame; the crisis would look little different with someone else at the head of the government, and certainly no better—not the defense chief, Yoav Gallant, nor the "opposition" leaders, Benny Gantz and Yair Lapid. None of these men depend on the war for their political survival, yet they all have endorsed its illegal and most lethal methods. The Israeli elite, regardless of its words, is bound by the same force it has unleashed. The Palestinian poet Mahmoud Darwish called it—during Israel's savage siege of Beirut in the summer of 1982—being "in the claws of the tank": trapped by the machinery on which you rely, the weapons you have made turned into a fetish of national salvation that is really a weapon for the destructions of nations and of people—your enemy's and your own.[9] It is a logic that regards the Palestinians as a "problem," and then only as a military problem; a logic that obliges those leaders to reach for the gun at first instinct. From the heights of a jet bomber or through the optics of a rifle, force that has failed is force that has not been applied firmly enough. And the machine, I. F. Stone once wrote, "is forgiven atrocities many-fold more terrible than those of the guerillas."[10]

The elites and their propagandists have a code word for the aggressive cascades of this horrid year, a useful euphemism. They call it "security." When the fighting is over, "security" is what Netanyahu wants to wield over what's left of Gaza's people.[11] The settler movement's conference in January was called "Settlement Brings Security."[12] For Bezalel Smotrich, champion of that movement, any talk of any ceasefire at any time serves only to "harm Israel's security."[13] To its patrons and armorers in Germany and the United States, "security" sounds reasonable and resounds with all those myths that have been so violently overthrown in the last twelve months but which they still believe in: restraint, self-defense, and, most deluded of all, "purity of arms"—the fable that holds the Israel Defense Forces to be the "most moral army in the world." For anyone who has ever faced the pointed end of this version of "security," they know its true meaning: domination and supremacy.

These constant spasms of savagery are an expression, strange though it may seem, of a profound vulnerability—a lack of real security. In the same way that negotiations were the only reliable method for returning hostages from Gaza and defending those locals still trapped there, a negotiated settlement—at last—is the only guarantor of safety. True safety, that is: the kind freed from fear and from anxiety, from a situation that requires you, periodically and with ever-increasing cruelty, to turn yourself and the soldiers you command into war criminals. It might take a generation; it might take two generations. Anyone with even a shade of the courage Israeli Prime Minister Yitzhak Rabin showed in the early 1990s—when he recognized the virtue of a political solution over endless bloodshed—will be killed just like he was, if the settlers have anything to say about it. Indeed, weeks before Rabin was murdered by a fascist in 1995, before the promise of the Oslo Accords was betrayed, Netanyahu had led a protest calling Rabin a "traitor."[14] If this is the insult thrown at those who would rather obey the warnings that for so long went unheeded, then we too should all be traitors. Better that than make yourself an accomplice.

CHAPTER ONE

SCOUR THE EARTH

When the High Priest and the Field Marshal Wear the Same Uniform

The Dreadnought, November 2023

"We are quite far from moral hesitations on the national battlefield. We see before us the command of the Torah, the most moral teaching in the world: Obliterate—until destruction." This instruction was published in August of 1943 in *He Hazit* (*The Front*), the house newsletter of a minor but vicious Jewish terror squad commanded by Avraham Stern.[1] For Stern and his posse, terrorism and revolutionary violence were not only the best method to liquidate the cops and bureaucrats then in charge of the British mandate in Palestine but a sacred duty: biblically warranted, a divine order from God. The order to "obliterate—until destruction" is an efficient paraphrase of 1 Samuel 15: "Thus said the Lord of Hosts: I am exacting the penalty . . . attack Amalek, and proscribe all that belongs to him. Spare no one, but kill alike men and women, infants and sucklings . . ." The specter of "Amalek" long ago lost its association with the nomadic tribe they once might have been and entered the religious imagination as an eternal enemy who can never be tolerated nor spared, the target of pitiless and never-ending revenge.

Three years before invoking the poor Amalekites in their underground war against the British, in 1940 Stern and his gang (known better by the Hebrew acronym Lehi) had broken with the hard right of the Zionist movement for being insufficiently cozy with the Nazis. Stern sent an envoy to Beirut to meet with fascist diplomats and stupidly wrote down his proposal for an alliance to throw out the British and establish, under German protection, a Jewish state on "totalitarian" lines.[2] Both Hitler and Stern, it seemed, could agree on more than just a Europe free of Jews.

During a brokered truce in 1948, Lehi members shot dead the UN mediator Folke Bernadotte in Jerusalem. Never mind that Bernadotte had arranged the liberation of hundreds of Jews from Theresienstadt during the war: he was a stooge and a heretic, an Amalek in tropical shorts. Lehi's chief of operations, who planned and ordered the assassination, was Yitzhak Shamir, later prime minister of Israel during the disastrous occupation of south Lebanon in the 1980s—a man who felt obliged to resign from Likud because Benjamin Netanyahu wasn't harsh enough in dealing with the Arabs.[3]

In 1986, during Shamir's second spell in office, Shmuel Derlich, chief rabbi of the Israeli army in Judea and Samaria (better known as the West Bank) sent a thousand-word letter to the troops under his care reminding them of their obligation to obey God's instruction if they ever met an "Amalekite." Asked who the Amalekites were supposed to represent in his missive, Derlich coyly replied "Germans." A lone crank, perhaps. But when Derlich was hauled before the judge advocate general he was defended publicly by forty other military chaplains.[4] Embedded deep in the army, even then, was the kind of inciting babble favored by Meir Kahane and his followers, their exemplar and icon today being Itamar Ben-Gvir, notorious for keeping an enormous mural of Baruch Goldstein in the lounge of his illegally built house in Kiryat Arba, east of Hebron. Ben-Gvir is the current minister of national security.[5]

Among the convoy of tanks and bulldozers bound south toward Gaza after October 7, you could find a one-eyed oldtimer: drowning in his reservist fatigues, barely able to hold on to his rifle, surrounded by the bracing cheers of young conscripts. This ninety-five-year-old was Ezra Yachin, and he was not there to fight but to instill in the troops "the spirit of the underground." Yachin, indeed, was in his youth a member of Lehi and happily participated in the pogrom at Deir Yassin in April of 1948 in which 110 Arab villagers were put to death.[6] "I stood them against a wall," recalled another Lehi fighter, referring to a pair of teenage girls, "and blasted them with two rounds from the Tommy gun."[7] The reference to the tommy gun is a nice reminder of who often serves as the armorer for this and other massacres, and it was at Deir Yassin and at the hands of men like Ezra Yachin that the pattern of the next three-quarters of a century was set.

His wattles drooping heavier by the day, Benjamin Netanyahu appeared on television on October 28 to announce the long-dreaded incursion by ground forces into Gaza and insist, as always: "the [Israel Defense Forces] is the most moral army in the world. The IDF does everything to avoid harming non-combatants."[8] A sickening glance at the tolls published by Gaza's ministry of health (which have always been reliable, contrary to slanders issued by the White House) will easily dismiss that bit of common fibbing: nearly 10,000 Palestinians slain (at the time of writing) by indiscriminate saturation bombing, a full third of them children.[9] To gird the nation and its soldiers for the slaughter to come, Netanyahu reached for scripture, quoting Deuteronomy (25:17–19). "Remember what Amalek did to you," he said, tactfully leaving out the next command: "Therefore, when your God grants you safety from all your enemies around you, in the land that your God is giving you as a hereditary portion, you shall blot out the memory of Amalek from under heaven."

Perhaps he trusts the pious and the faithful enough to work out the rest on their own, to follow the eradication of a people with the eradication of their memory. Perhaps he means for us to be relieved when he appeals only to biblical warrants for extermination and doesn't, as his colleague Yoav Gallant did, explicitly describe a captive civilian population as animals worthy of slaughter. Perhaps he hopes we might be deceived by his resort to the hollow clichés of the security state and fail to notice that at work here is a deep-held desire: not just that the high priest and the field marshal should wear the same uniform, but that they should be *the same person*. This potent blend of vengeful violence with messianic zeal has never been the dominant tendency in the Zionist movement (usually it's just the former), but it has always been there—a tar-dark and hardened heart—and the further rightward you tack, the closer you get to the grubby supremacist impulse, the faster that heart beats. Netanyahu—corrupt down to his socks—now heads the most virulently nationalist and orthodox government in the country's history, a government which takes blessings for its revenge from on high and acts like the revenant ghost of Avraham Stern.

In the face of their own immense and indissoluble grief, as they bury their own children, a majority of the Israeli public (if the polls are to be believed) are refusing to concede. Many Israelis, it should be remembered, spent much of last winter in the streets of Haifa and Tel Aviv trying to topple the government. It only took seventy-five years, but the middle class were finally beginning to realize that the barbed-wire and machine-gun-nest system built on the nation's periphery, in the settlements and watchtowers of the state, was always going to fold back in on itself. The regime built to control Palestinian existence, this regime which Jacob Abolafia memorably called "a cabinet of settler-ministers," turned around to face its internal enemies—the judiciary, the universities, the electoral commission, the left—and was met with insurrectionary defiance.[10] This spirit refuses to fade in the tempest of atrocity, and most Israelis (including the families of hostages taken on October 7) still demand an all-for-all exchange of prisoners and have placed their excoriating blame for the horrors of that day firmly on Netanyahu's desk.[*]

---

[*] If opinion polls are to be trusted at all, it is in the aggregate over a long stretch of time. And what those polls consistently showed for more than a year was a majority of the Israeli population believing *not enough violence was being inflicted on Gaza*. I retain this paragraph here only as a record of the mood and impression in early November 2023, and the recollection of a hope—for Israelis to overthrow their butchers' government by force—which was later soundly disproven.

And they are right. Netanyahu now finds himself—when not approving the double-tapping of Gazan hospitals—obliged to destroy the same entity he helped to prop up for the last fourteen years. Since returning to power in 2009, Netanyahu's doctrine has been to split the Palestinian movement geographically as well as politically so as to avoid ever having to talk about negotiations—negotiations which, should they ever reach any level of seriousness, would inevitably have to discuss the tearing down of illegal settlements.[11] To achieve this split Netanyahu made sure to keep Hamas firmly in power, and with a divided Palestinian leadership he could claim the occupied population lacked a unified representative. One could argue that by their war of expulsion against Fatah after the elections in 2006, Hamas made the political split a reality. Yet it was Netanyahu who ensured that split would remain permanent. To this end he allowed the Qataris to send US$1 billion to Gaza between 2012 and 2018, half of which ended up in the hands of Hamas and its militias. The result, as sharply described by the historian Dmitry Shumsky in a column for *Haaretz*, was to turn

> Hamas from a minor terrorist organization into an efficient, lethal army with highly trained, dehumanized stormtroopers. . . . An Israeli prime minister himself knowingly and calculatingly cultivated one of Israel's most bitter and fanatic foes, an enemy whose declared aim is to destroy the country. And he did it to prevent the horror scenario from his standpoint of a return to Israeli-Palestinian negotiations. Netanyahu recklessly gambled on the lives of Israelis,

and in fact, last Shabbat, more than 1,000 of them
paid the price of that foolish gamble with their lives.[12]

In a comprehensive survey of opinion in the Strip published in *Foreign Affairs* (taken before October 7), well
over half of Gazans declared they had little trust in
Hamas as a governing party or in Hamas's ability to secure
Palestinian freedom.[13] The shameless and hollow inverse of
Netanyahu's scheming has been to saddle the Palestinians
in Gaza with an authority that does not represent them,
does not tend to their needs, and chooses instead to send
its "martyrs" into settlements to behead kibbutzniks with
shovels.

"Mowing the grass" is the grotesque euphemism used in
the IDF to describe the regular and rhythmic use of overwhelming force against Gaza (more grotesque even than the
names the army gives to its operations: Cast Lead, Pillar of
Defense, Protective Edge). We are well beyond that now.
The Israeli government, not content with keeping its annihilatory violence within the boundaries of the river and the
sea, thinks it wise to export it overseas. It was Israeli arms
shipments, flying by schedule from the military airbase at
Ovda, which allowed the army of Azerbaijan to evict at
gunpoint the Armenian population of Nagorno Karabakh
in September.[14] *This is the method; this is the goal.* Planning
documents leaked to the press speak confidently of a deliberate expulsion of the entire citizenry of Gaza to the Sinai and
a "sterile zone" built between the disposed Palestinians and
their old, flattened homes.[15] Yet in pursuing this and other
murderous goals, any cabinet of settler-ministers will inevitably find themselves in defiance of God's holy instructions.

Because it is impossible to truly "blot out the memory" of a people. No matter how total the crime, no matter how complete the cleansing, the memory always remains.

CHAPTER TWO

EVEN IF THE PEOPLE PERISH

The Cultural Destruction of Gaza

New Republic, March 2024

Gaza might soon be a land without a past. Israeli bombardment from land and air has been so thorough and discriminate that whatever Gazans can claim as their distinct cultural inheritance and artistic achievement is now either rubble and ruin or under serious threat. The Municipal Library is gone.[1] The Central Archives facility has been gutted completely; burned inside was a century's documentary evidence of Gaza's urban development.[2] The Edward Said Library, with its English-language collection, is likely a ruin too.[3] Souq Al Zawiya, Gaza's oldest continuous market in the Old City, has been evaporated.[4] The only museum in Rafah is a mass of electrical cabling and dust; little remains of the grand Pasha Palace, where Napoleon once stopped during his Egyptian campaign.[5] The modern Palace of Justice, home of Gaza's court system, was deliberately demolished in early December.[6] Sometimes Israeli targeting seems churlishly spiteful. The Rashad Al Shawa Center had a theater for films and musicians, stained glass above its central hall, and a small library. It was here, in 1998, with Bill Clinton in the audience, that the Palestine Liberation Organization voted to remove from its charter all references to the destruction of Israel. That fact did not spare the place; the Center is now a husk.[7]

Early in his thinking Raphael Lemkin, who invented the theory of genocide in 1943 after fleeing the advance of Nazi forces into his native Poland, thought a people's artistic, religious, literary, and iconographic heritage was vital to their thriving, and that to wipe it out completely would still count as a vast crime even if the plunderers left the people alive. He called such an act "vandalism," later, "cultural genocide," and like most of his better ideas, it did not survive the abattoir of secretarial drafts and committee debates on its way to codification in the 1948 Genocide Convention. Lemkin's cosmopolitanism—though naïve and born from the false promise of a right to a homeland in someone else's home—was motivated by the romantic idea that humankind in all its forms was capable of majesty. In pursuit of its own permanence, importance, or glory, every society built its monoliths and megastructures, its temples and statues, and each in turn gifted something of value to the human whole. The defiling of one monument, one altar, one library was therefore an assault on all libraries, all altars, all monuments. Cultural expression was shared expression, universal, and bound in a common trove.

There has been much fraught talk of intent since Israel appeared before the International Court of Justice charged with genocide. Just how tightly has the siege on the Strip been held? With what foreknowledge did military commanders continue to cut off the enclaves and exclaves Palestinians were told were safe from shrapnel and strafing? Yet outside the courtroom, intent matters little; the accumulated effect of Israeli actions is enough to judge their morality. Taken with the gruesomely high death toll—two-thirds of which is made up by children and women—the extreme vandalism visited upon Gaza's cultural identity speaks in only one direction: a determination to make Palestinian life just another subterranean strata, one more vanished civilization under the rubble to be poked and peered at as a curio many years into a darker future; a lost society to join all the others.

Like everywhere else in the Mediterranean basin, Gaza's scarred soil sits atop that of other civilizations, and its compounded layers reach down and back to the earliest examples of human settlement. Beneath its landmarks rest the landmarks of earlier ages; a sandstone wall traces the track of a much earlier edifice made of mudbrick. The Great Omari Mosque in the Old City, Gaza's largest religious site, was once Roman, then Byzantine, transformed by early Muslims and Abbasids, conquered by Crusaders, passing between Mamluk glory and Mongol ravages, restored by the Ottomans, damaged by the British (Crusaders, again), lately entering Palestinian life as the epicenter and emblem of Gaza's endurance.[8] Not much of it remains now but a few arches. In December, the octagonal minaret stood, stripped down to its base by Israeli shelling. By late January, the tower was cleaved in half.[9]

It is no relief to know the bombing is nondenomina-
tional; Israeli gunners are just as content splitting open
churches as mosques. Nearly 500 people were sheltering
under the eaves of Saint Porphyrius when an Israeli missile
struck it on October 19. Among the eighteen killed was
Marwan Tarazi, custodian of the vast, vibrant archive of pic-
tures taken by the famous Palestinian-Armenian photographer Kegham Djeghalian between the 1940s and 1970s.[10]
Djeghalian liked scenes of everyday life: family picnics under
the citrus groves, fez-topped suited men drinking coffee on
the boardwalk, shopkeepers watching from their stalls. The
ordinary tedium of the working day looks miraculous when
seen from the wreckage.[11]

We are told, and told again, to consider Israeli crimes
as excesses, to treat its army's barbarism as regrettable over-
reach. This is what happens in war, plead Israel's dutiful
linebackers; savagery must be met in kind, goes the cynical
and weary lament. "Whoever dares to accuse our soldiers of
war crimes are hypocritical liars who lack so much as one
drop of morality," Netanyahu said in his infamous "Amalek"
remarks. "The IDF is the most moral army in the world."
No bomb or shell is unleashed on hospital or museum,
we're reassured, without good intelligence of an enemy
cache or bunker or tunnel. Such tortured logic has its limits. The artillery damage to the 1,600-year-old St. Hilarion
monastery complex—the oldest Christian site of its kind in
the Middle East—was clearly inflicted because the plastic
roof covering the ruins provides excellent cover from JDAM
guided bombs.[12] The Greek-era site of Anthedon Harbour
with its cemetery and seaside ramparts needed to be fired
upon in case it was used as a tactical defensive position.[13] The

Al Sammara bathhouse in Zeitoun, probably dating from the fourteenth century, was obviously obliterated because Hamas fighters were caught sweltering in their towels.[14]

Kill the past, kill the future. Pride, inspiration, curiosity, passion—these are the emotions curtailed when you cut a people off from the roots of their land, when you shatter every place where those same emotions might be fulfilled. The Israeli army has made learning of any kind an impossibility. According to United Nations statistics, around 625,000 school-age children remain in Gaza, and not a single one of them has a place where they can study or be taught. In UN parlance, the total eradication of every school in Gaza is diplomatically called "no access to education."[15]

What goes for children goes for adults, though only they can grasp the scale of what has been stripped from them. Israa University was opened in 2014 with a special emphasis on scholarships for the poor. Sixty-five percent of its students were women. "Poverty," Dr. Ahmed Alhussaina, Israa's vice president, told *The Intercept*, "would not stand as an obstacle in front of any Palestinian that wants to pursue a college degree."[16] The campus was kept intact longer than any of Gaza's other universities because it was occupied as an IDF command post for two months; in mid-January, Israa was flattened to the cheers of watching troops. The 3,000 artifacts from Gaza's pre-Islamic past in its collection were either looted or pulverized. The divisional commander responsible for bringing it down, Barak Hiram, was later censured for doing so without higher sanction—permission the commander's superiors would have given anyway: "If you had submitted the request to collapse the university for my approval," Major General Yaron Finkelman informed Hiram, "I would have approved it."[17]

In early January, an IDF soldier named Yishai Shalev (a hairdresser in civilian life) filmed a video of himself: "For all those asking why there is no education in Gaza . . ." He pans over his shoulder. Beyond lies the shattered frontage of Al Azhar University, an open blast wound in its right flank. "Oops," says Shalev. "We've had a missile fall on them. That sucks. Too bad. That's how you'll never be engineers anymore."[18] "Never" is the critical word here, for what such free and easy destruction teaches Gazans in the absence of their own schools and colleges is futility. No matter what you build, Israel warns, it will be brought down; no matter how much you might wish to improve yourself and your lot, it will be stripped from you; no matter how nobly you strive to distinguish yourself from the philistine nihilists of Hamas, we will treat you like them anyway. Look upon my works, they instruct, and despair.

In the persistent pattern of cultural vandalism, you can catch a hint of frustration on the part of the destroyers. There's an old Zionist slogan or talking point, sometimes still repeated in public by the ignorant or belligerent, that Palestine isn't really a nation with a history of its own; that its people are just another flavor of Arab who could live any-where else. This was never true, and even in the neglect of places like the Omari Mosque and the Pasha Palace due to lack of funding for restoration work and a lack of building supplies, their durability represents Gaza's own unique his-tory, distinct even from Jerusalem, Jaffa, and Jenin. But war is the zone where will meets possibility. Netanyahu always had the will but often lacked the possibility. Just as he acted for years to keep the Palestinian leadership in both territories divided—propping up Hamas at the expense of Fatah secularists in the West Bank—so as to foreclose the emergence of a united nation, he acts now to eradicate the very foundations on which a future nation could be built.

In peace and war cultural property is supposed to be immune from attack, protected by the second protocol of the 1954 Hague Convention. It has not shielded anything in Gaza, nor did it stop Eli Eskozido, the head of the Israel Antiquities Authority, from sending his deputy to inspect a warehouse in Gaza stacked with fragile artifacts (controlled jointly by the Palestinian Antiquities Office and the École Biblique et Archéologique Française). Eskozido then bravely published a video of soldiers at the site online (with the comic book caption "Wow!") accompanied by a photo of dozens of pieces displayed in glass cases in the lobby of the Knesset.[19] Eskozido deleted the video; the Israeli Antiquities Authority denied taking anything from the storeroom. No one but the Israelis know how many objects have been stolen from Gaza.

Both the glories and the detritus of antiquity tell us: Even if the people perish, their works and monuments still remain. Survivors of past cataclysms warn us: Even if their works and monuments are shattered, the people still remember. What happens, though, when both treasure and treasurer are effaced from the earth, when life and history are condemned as equally perishable, when souls and spoils are weighed, measured, and judged alike as equally disposable?

Treasures are everything in a land deprived of everything but treasures. A jag of Umayyad pottery can sate no hunger, a purse of Roman denarii entombed for two millennia will not keep the lights on, but these emblems are good reasons to go on surviving, to persist when everything around you speaks only of death. A turquoise mosaic on a mosque wall, a gold-tinged fresco on a chapel vault, the leaf-fringed curve of a Hellenic urn—all stoke the dream of a time when their admirers might not be threatened by bombs and tanks, in a secure nation, proof at last of a people's worthiness to exist and live unmolested in the lands of their birth.

CHAPTER THREE

RAMBO IN THE STERILE ZONE
The Settlers' Plan for Gaza

New Republic, February 2024

For the Israeli settler movement, Hamas's bloody October 7 incursion presented an opportunity. Barely two months into the Israel Defense Forces' scouring of the Gaza Strip, the inner core of the movement gathered in a hall in the port town of Ashdod. They did not wear yellow ribbons, the color of solidarity with the hostages, and did not devote themselves to prayers for the hostages' return. They wore orange and prayed for a different restoration: a reconquest of Gaza, the expansion of the Greater Land of Israel, and the dispossession of an entire people.[1]

The Ashdod meeting, on November 22, foreshadowed an orgy of incitement at the International Convention Center in Jerusalem on January 28—a coming-out shindig for a revived front that binds together settler matriarch Daniella Weiss's group, Nachala; the dregs of the old terrorist underground, in the form of convicted (though pardoned) militant Uzi Sharbag; mainline Likudniks; and the semi-fascist Jewish Power and Religious Zionist parties.[2] The garish T-shirts, the fridge magnets, the jubilant bouncing all hailed an emboldened attitude: that the populace of Gaza should not be treated as a people—with the bare functional minimum of rights—but as an obstacle to be crudely trampled. While their immediate motives might be bloodlust or free real estate, the political goal is to make their ascendancy and power permanent. "This is our final opportunity to rebuild and expand the land of Israel," the Likud minister Haim Katz warned.[3] Political will is aligning with real possibility, and the air is thick with the plague-smell of postwar planning. None of it includes the Palestinians.[4]

For example, on January 10, Yinon Magal—who was once in the same hard-right party as Israeli Finance Minister Bezalel Smotrich and fantasized on air about machine-gunning fellow journalists "like Rocky" (he meant Rambo)—shared a proposal and petition supposedly compiled by residents of the Gaza Envelope, the protective circle of towns Hamas pierced in October.[5] Under this scheme, Palestinian territory would be compressed to two tiny, separate districts around Khan Younis and Deir al Balah, the rest of the Strip ringed by a kilometer-thick military zone, the northernmost districts given over to an industrial park and a seaside boardwalk. Beach strolls for Jews; ghettos for the rest.[6] That the accompanying petition has barely scraped 3,000 signatures does not matter; its authors act to please God, not the electorate.[7]

Foreign Minister Israel Katz, meanwhile, used valuable time in front of Europe's top diplomats not to endorse an enduring political settlement but to pitch a Gulf State–style boondoggle: an artificial island dredged from the Gazan coast as a "commercial hub" for trade. Of what use an off-shore port would be to a people without a home, Katz did not care to explain—nor did he seem to appreciate the coastline was not his to develop. (The European Union apparatchiks who had to sit through this video presentation were "perplexed"—diplomat-speak for "extremely pissed off.")[8]

Roughly two million Palestinians remain in Gaza. Their existence is daily becoming more tortured and desperate, but they are still large enough as a mass to seriously stall the settlers' return. There are plans for that too. The Intelligence Ministry, which offers nonbinding advice to the Israeli government, suggested in a policy document (just five days after the Hamas offensive) that the entire population be expelled to a "sterile zone" in the Sinai Desert. Parallel propaganda efforts would make it "clear that there is no hope of returning." The Misgav Institute—a right-wing think tank linked to Likud—published a similar proposal for the forced "transfer" of the entire population. Apparently the tiny messianist group Build Israel somehow managed to put its own paper in front of American lawmakers—including AIPAC ally Joe Wilson, a Republican congressman from South Carolina—suggesting that foreign aid to countries like Iraq and Turkey be made conditional on their accepting thousands of Palestinian refugees.[9] In a statement accompanying the plan, the plotters said these would be the "correct, moral and humane avenues for the relocation of the Gazan population."

At all points it is taken for granted that fewer Palestinians—not counting those already slain—will live in their homeland once the Israelis are through with them. To call this "moral and humane" or a "voluntary migration" smells of preemptive self-defense against the shackles of international law. But you can trust the settlers and their allies to say what others wouldn't dare. At the Jerusalem conference in January, Israeli Communications Minister Shlomo Karhi described exactly and clearly what they mean: "'Voluntary,'" Karhi explained, is "a state you impose [on someone] until they give their consent."[10]

If Benjamin Netanyahu had proposed any concrete plans for Gaza's future, there would be room for fewer wild annihilatory schemes from others. He has not. No doubt when the government does unveil its proposal, it will contain the cruelty so openly displayed elsewhere, simply sheathed in the salving language of appeasement and reasonableness. It is in this gap that the settler movement operates. "Netanyahu left us an opening," Daniella Weiss said in January. "He invites this pressure." And it is from Weiss and her close colleague Yossi Dagan, the West Bank overlord, that the real threat comes. When they publish their maps, pins carefully placed on Gaza City, Khan Younis, and Rafah, their intent is backed by decades of experience as the deniable, unofficial, paramilitary arm of Israel's nation-building project.

In one of the government's few clear statements of postwar intent, Defense Minister Yoav Gallant, freshly censured by the International Court of Justice, said Israel would not reoccupy Gaza.[11] Promises like these, of course, are made to be broken; he also insisted on "military freedom of operation"—a security regime very much like that in the West Bank, which makes life hellish for Palestinians and emboldens the settlers who supplant them.[12] The clearance of Palestinians from their homes and farms in Judea and Samaria usually begins with the designation of territory as "survey land," "state land," "closed military zones," or "firing zones"—categories approved by the courts and enforced by the army.[13] In a morbid sense, this typical faux-legal process has already been achieved in Gaza by dumb bombs and dynamite, no orders or writs required.

Any buffer region or defense line ringing the postwar Strip is precisely the zone coveted by settlers as the incubator for a new phase of *reconquista*, reapplying their methods and training from around Jenin and Hebron onto a pulverized and deracinated land flushed of its people. Here they can run up their outposts and blockhouses, to be followed by walled enclaves, and create a fait accompli: a network of exurbs and garrison towns laced with critical infrastructure like highways, water treatment plants, and power lines the police and the army have no choice but to defend. "Bullshit," said the ex-Mossad chief Tamir Pardo in response to the conference's subtitle, "Settlement Brings Security." "They don't defend us," he said, "we have to defend them."[14] Which is precisely the point.

The IDF is a backstop. Kitted out with state-issued rifles, the settlers live for the chance to provoke confrontations that are the pretext for the seizure of yet more land, yet more blood. "Continuous, systematic violence meted out by settlers," B'Tselem has said, "is part of Israel's official policy, driving massive takeover of Palestinian farmland and pastureland."[15] It is apt indeed for our neoliberal

age—and an ironic inversion of Israel's tech start-up economy—that the leading edge of the state's brutality should
be "outsourced," as the academic Tareq Baconi puts it, "to
its colonial pioneers." Such a method "is not a breakdown
of the state's monopoly on violence; it is the delegation of
that violence to enforcers on the frontier."[16] The settlers
have anointed themselves sentinels of the borderlands, both
the lookouts and vanguard of the state even as they rebel,
with God-given arrogance, against the nation they hope to
enlarge.

The settlers' political wing is much more visible and potent
than it was in 2005, when troops were sent to clear settlements like Gush Katif as part of the Sharon government's "disengagement" from Gaza. In the Knesset, usual suspects like
Smotrich and National Security Minister Itamar Ben-Gvir are
aided in their attempt to amend the Disengagement Law to
allow free movement of Israelis in Gaza by several mainline
Likudniks.[17] Ben-Gvir, meanwhile, is just as content pulling
a handgun on protesters as he is threatening to withdraw his
Jewish Power Party from the emergency government and collapse Netanyahu's coalition.[18] Types like these are not a dissi-
dent strain; they are the spokesmen of an ideology encultured
in the settlements now circling back and entering the main-
stream.[19] Present at the January conference: almost half of the
governing coalition and five sitting ministers.

Nevertheless, we're told to pay no heed to the cranks
and lunatics. They're just charlatans, these settlers, noisy but
inconsequential; worry not, and listen to the adults in the
room. "Israel is not about to rebuild any settlements in the
Gaza Strip," said the Israeli journalist Anshel Pfeffer, leading light of the liberal and secular school; the polls don't

support them, anyway—as if opinion polling (or democracy) mattered to people who want to hasten the dawn of Judgment Day. Meanwhile, American officials aver that they are very "troubled" by settler threats and "unequivocal" in their opposition to them, which is to say—not that bothered. The Biden administration thought about sanctioning Ben-Gvir and Smotrich. Instead, it kicked that can very hard down a dark path.[20]

It is little comfort to know that every one of these bullish statements made by a settler-minister will end up on the charge sheet of The Hague, evidence of Israel's breach of the provisional order not to incite genocide. The settlers continue to act as if international and domestic law were as relevant as Palestinian lives. In their two-front war against the secularity of the Israeli state and against Palestinian nationhood, they are plotting for a "speedy end," as Bezalel Smotrich put it in his deranged "Decisive Plan," published in 2017: a cap on the phase of "conflict management" that has seen Netanyahu forestall self-determination efforts for decades at the price of instability, and a complete closure on the possibility of a just settlement. "Full Israeli sovereignty," Smotrich demands. "Any solution must be based on cutting off the ambition to realize the Arab national hope between the Jordan and the Mediterranean."[21] Talk of "solutions" implying the eradication or displacement of a people brings up the nastiest of historical memories, and it is verging on tasteless to stick "final" in front of that term. But when Smotrich and the settlers say they want this state of affairs to be "irreversible," it is difficult to think of anything else.

CHAPTER FOUR

WHERE'S DADDY?
The Methods of Destruction

New Republic, April 2024

It has long been true in political life, as the old saying goes, that the scandal is never what is illegal but what is allowed. Only now, six months into the Gazan nightmare, are we finally beginning to grasp the harsh contours of Israeli methods. What this picture reveals is not the saturnalia sometimes evoked in desperate protests against the war—a mirror of October 7, only in uniform—but a coldly vengeful abandoning of restraint and a super-technological dismemberment, piece by gory piece, of Palestinian existence. The worst examples puked up by history have not made their debut—there has been no carpet-bombing, no roaming death squads—but what can be seen is an array of techniques, each as deadly as the last, notable for how they can be excused and disguised as conforming to international law.

In this sense the most vital and fearsome unit in the Israeli army is not the jacked-up naval commandos of Shayetet 13 nor even the shady spooks, Unit 8200; it is the International Law Department of the Military Advocate General's Corps. The department's daily work is to paste a veneer of properness and decorum over Israel Defense Forces operations, and its responsibilities are the opposite of what they appear. Far from binding the army to a strict code, the department carefully molds the gaps through which a bomber pilot can fly with his murderous load. Instead of jailing killers and torturers, it defends them. The deceptiveness of its advice allows the top brass to swing contentedly in their swivel chairs at IDF headquarters and gives comfort to the common private, safe in the knowledge that unless he does something particularly stupid—like triple-strike a protected aid convoy—he will keep his job.[1] The ILD's sober advice permits Benjamin Netanyahu and Defense chief Yoav Gallant to believe they are not lying when they say on TV that their country does not deliberately kill civilians. Last, and most importantly, the ILD's guidance permits Israel's defenders in Britain, Germany, and the United States to prop themselves at the dais and give their banal reasons for why the slaughter will not stop.

Very early in the war, before the ground campaign began and when the bulk of destruction fell to the air force, it was the International Law Department that obliterated the principle of proportionality—the slightly foggy rule that says the value of a military action must be weighed against the potential for civilian harm. Usually this is formulated as a ratio: five innocents for one combatant, say. The IDF gave itself permission to use formulas of 15-to-1 or

20-to-1—even for the lowest-ranking members of Hamas.[2]
According to Israeli journalist Yuval Abraham's thorough
and terrifying reports in +972 magazine, the army relied on
two "artificial intelligence" systems, Lavender and Gospel,
to provide targeting data.[3] Traditional methods—human
labor, due diligence—were too slow to keep pace with the
thirst for revenge; "just a few seconds" was all it took to
"verify" a target, a check that often consisted of nothing
more than noticing whether the victim was a man rather
than a woman. As one of Abraham's sources says of the
International Law Department's instructions: "They directly
tell you: 'You are allowed to kill [Hamas fighters] along with
many civilians.'"[*]

Like all such systems, Lavender and Gospel are neither
"artificial" nor "intelligent." They cannot think for themselves and only sort the information fed into them faster
than a person could. Such machines inevitably spit out a
mirror image of their masters, beliefs and prejudices intact.
Lavender was "more likely to select civilians by mistake
when its algorithms were applied to the general population," Abraham reports. When "no uninvolved civilians"
is the catchphrase of the entire military-political apparatus
from the common private up to President Isaac Herzog, the
machine believes it too.[4]

---

* The extremely high "collateral damage" ratio of 20 to 1 applied
only to low-ranking fighters. To target Hamas commanders and
leaders, the figure was much higher, the area marked for bombing
far wider. Further reporting by Yuval Abraham in +972 *Magazine*
revealed the ratio could be as high as 100 to 1 or *even 300 to 1*.
To kill Osama Bin Laden, for reference, the US military allowed a
"non-combat casualty cut-off value" of just thirty.

Another machine, called "Where's Daddy?" is designed
to alert its operator when a potential target is at home. The
real perversity of the system—more than its sick name—is
in revealing the nonsense of Israel's own propaganda claims:
that it is difficult to fight Hamas cleanly because its fighters use apartments, mosques, and hospitals as a shield. The
army routinely bombs homes to target fighters because it
is easier than finding them in the street.[5] Just as routinely,
there is a gap between when the system identifies a target at
home and when the ordnance is dropped; the bombers do
not always know for sure if the true target is struck but are
certain of inevitable civilian deaths. Strikes on homes are
usually done with "dumb bombs." These munitions do not
have precision equipment, their weight made up instead
with extra explosive. When no place is safe, families shel-
ter together. As a result, families are eradicated together.
The International Law Department's allowance of twenty
or more civilians slain in exchange for the mere possibility
of killing a single target disgusted enough officers that they
blew the whistle on the technology and the mentality that
made family annihilation a de facto common policy.*

---

* At this point in the war, only the existence of Lavendar, Gospel,
and Where's Daddy? had been revealed. Unit 8200's real suite of
programs is larger still. According to the IDF, "'Alchemist" can
predict terrorist attacks. "Depth of Wisdom" maps Hamas's tunnel network. "Hunter and Flow" allows for querying of different
datasets (see "Israel built an 'AI factory' for war. It unleashed it in
Gaza," *Washington Post*, December 29, 2024). Google, Microsoft,
and Amazon have all allowed the IDF to use its technology,
including the storage of classified information on cloud servers (see
"Militarised AI," *London Review of Books* blog, January 28, 2024).

Another common practice is the use of a "combat zone" or "kill zone"—a deadly radius around an army unit's dug-in position.[6] Anything or anyone entering this zone is shot or shelled. No signposts or banners mark the outer rim, and there is no forewarning of the kind the IDF boasted about during the war's earlier air campaign. No one truly knows how many innocents have been slaughtered in these zones; the picture is distorted by the army's method of classifying slain civilian men as "terrorists" in after-action reports, and few soldiers are willing or able to check if the details are true. One of the rare clues as to how troops operate in these zones is found in the case of the three Israeli hostages—shirtless, speaking Hebrew, waving a white flag—who wandered unknowingly into a zone and were killed on sight. The army's own investigation revealed that the last to die was shot by a soldier who disobeyed a direct "cease fire" order from a superior.[7] Some units, it seems, make up their own rules. Volunteer surgeons and nurses working in the few remaining functional hospitals report a "steady stream" of children trolleyed onto wards (or straight to the morgue) with single wounds to the head and torso, often from high-caliber ammunition. They too have been shot while clutching white cloths—evidence of sharpshooters, who, by definition, work alone and far from the shackles of good conduct.[8]

When a three-car World Central Kitchen convoy laden with food aid set out from a warehouse in Deir al Balah on April 1, its volunteer workers went by the reasonable belief that Israeli soldiers would not "go rogue." They did not survive long enough to mourn the futility of such an assumption. The trucks were clearly marked, and the aid team had cleared its route with the army beforehand and gained a promise they would be safe. And still the convoy was struck three different times along a 1.5-mile stretch of coastal road—all because the drone operators claimed to suspect someone with them might be armed, a person they knew never left the warehouse.[9] Though commanders sacked the soldiers responsible, the habit of firing at anything judged to be suspicious—on a whim, on a hunch, without any kind of rubber stamp—appears to be encultured in the army, a smug belief that even if soldiers break the strictest rules, they will not face a consequence. This was true of the general who dynamited Israa University without higher approval—approval that would have been given if he asked.

It is something of a cliché to say that the nonenforcement of the law leads inevitably to impunity; punish every crime equally or, in time, no crime will be punishable. In the Israeli case, this axiom is undeniable. In 2017, the brave human rights group B'Tselem was warning against the brutal policing and settlement of the occupied West Bank, a persistent pattern of violence driven in part by the unwillingness of military police and the courts to punish transgression of the code Israel swears it lives and dies by. It would lead, B'Tselem insisted, to more brutality more often. The army's most murderous actions, even then,

> were justified based on a formalistic adherence to [international humanitarian law] and to an expansive interpretation of these rules, to the point where they are drained of all meaning and substance. This conduct, which has caused thousands of casualties, has

been largely ignored by the military law enforcement system. In most cases, no investigation is opened at all; in the rare cases that are investigated, no further action is taken. Other than a handful of cases, usually involving low-ranking soldiers, no one has been put on trial.[10]

Now, in more extreme circumstances than the West Bank seven years ago, the ILD's rules of engagement are thinner than a communion wafer and as pliable as a plastic bag. The rules have, by their permissiveness, transformed every soul in Gaza into a viable target, a potential victim, and the land itself into a free-fire zone. And every day John Kirby, US national security spokesman, will appear coolly before their mutilated faces and swear some variation on the common theme: "To date," Kirby said on April 2, we "have not found any incidents where the Israelis have violated international humanitarian law."[11]

One of the few beautiful qualities of law is its capacity to run both ways: It guards the potential victim from harm as well as potential perpetrators from debasing themselves. Every time the Israeli army and the whole political edifice that supports it permits an atrocity, it coarsens itself, makes itself a prisoner of its own cruelty. Cease now, before there is nothing left to salvage.

CHAPTER FIVE

IN THE DOCK, PART I

Israel's Threats at the International Court of Justice

New Republic, January 2024

In their often shambolic and occasionally hysterical appearance before the International Court of Justice last Friday, at no point did the lawyers representing Israel give concrete arguments or convincing evidence that their state's three-month siege of Gaza should not be considered an act of genocide. Faced with a credible accusation of a crime one of their own called the "epitome and zenith of evil," "the crime of crimes," "the ultimate in wickedness," they produced no proof they were not guilty.[1]

Though they trumpeted the aid Israel is allegedly allowing into Gaza, Israel's lawyers could not answer how it came to be that more than a million Palestinians will soon face outright famine.[2] The Israel Defense Forces have to confront Hamas wherever they find its fighters, the lawyers insisted.

But that cannot explain why a full 45 percent of Gaza's housing stock is now a gray ruin or why entire city blocks are dynamited long after the area is cleared of the enemy; why indeed some of the oldest churches and mosques in the world are now husks.[3] Proclaiming the high moral goal of rescuing hostages and insisting at every turn that the IDF obeys the rules of war, the lawyers gave no account for why Israeli soldiers felt able and entitled to shoot their own on sight. Yotam Haim, Samer Talalka, and Alon Shamriz: three men, shirtless, speaking Hebrew, waving a white flag.[4] The leaflet drops, the text messages, the voicemails: This strategy of forewarning Gaza's civilians was held up as an example of the army's duty to international law, though no rebuttal was offered for why unguided "dumb" bombs are dropped on the very towns and villages and camps Palestinians were told were safe from strike—the same places those leaflets informed them would guarantee their lives.

Instead, Israel's lawyers and agents complained. The charge of genocide brought by South Africa in The Hague was "a libel" designed to "delegitimize" the Israeli state and society. South Africa, which gave its submission to the court on Thursday, was seeking to "weaponize" the Genocide Convention in a "concerted and cynical attempt to pervert" the law's true purpose. The lawyers, each in their turn, performed the usual acts of contrition and hand-wringing for the victims of so-called collateral damage: the "tragic . . . heartbreaking . . . terrible" civilian death toll that it attributed not to the designs and intent of the military but to the "harsh realities" of urban combat.

South Africa is seeking urgent "provisional measures"— an emergency ruling from the court based on the plausibility or possibility of a genocide taking place. South Africa had to prove Israel has a prima facie case to answer. In these preliminary hearings, there is no burden of proof. Evidence is not checked, witnesses are not called, facts are not validated. Truth, at this stage, does not matter. The Israeli team must have been thrilled. Galit Raguan, stressing at all times the IDF's difficulty fighting in civilian areas used by Hamas for cover, baldly claimed that "hospitals have not been bombed." The World Health Organization has meanwhile documented six hundred attacks on Gaza hospitals, clinics, and ambulances since October; there is no functioning hospital at all in Gaza's north.[5] Raguan later pointed proudly to a picture of an IDF soldier holding a handgun allegedly found in an incubator for newborns, as if a single pistol would justify the shelling of the hospital it was found in—an attack that according to her never happened. Earlier, Tal Becker, a legal adviser to Israel's Ministry of Foreign Affairs, stated that Raphael Lemkin— the deeply flawed and compromised architect of the theory of genocide—"witnessed the unspeakable horrors of the Holocaust." Lemkin did not; he was in the United States by 1941. On such shaky ground, it was very brave for Becker to then argue that South Africa's eighty-four-page, tightly argued written submission to the International Court of Justice (ICJ), sourced and footnoted almost exclusively from UN documents, was "curated, decontextualized, and manipulative."[6]

The defects of the Genocide Convention run deep. Unlike a charge of common murder or even crimes against humanity, and contrary to our impression of the breadth of its protection, the Convention does not shield everyone: Certain groups, such as ethnic or religious minorities, can be victims, but anyone outside that boundary—political groups, say, or the disabled—do not qualify. Trickier still, it demands prosecutors prove the perpetrator's "intent to destroy," an almost impossibly high bar to clear, for a genocidaire rarely brandishes his own smoking gun. What South Africa had to demonstrate on Thursday was an equation: clear expressions of intent plus a persistent pattern of atrocity. Since October 7, and since the order was given for a bombardment without precision or mercy, Israeli leaders have been determined to make that equation easier to solve.

When Prime Minister Benjamin Netanyahu implored the troops and the nation to "remember what Amalek did to you," he was citing a biblical argument for acting indiscriminately, and his colleagues have dutifully followed this pattern of collapsing the crucial distinction between civilian and combatant, between war and vengeance. "We will eliminate everything," said Defense Minister Yoav Gallant, erasing the line between Hamas and not-Hamas.[*] Finance

---

[*]   A week after the ICJ hearings, when Gallant's words were used extensively in South Africa's presentation to evoke intent to commit genocide, Yair Rosenberg in *The Atlantic* magazine (January 21, 2024) claimed that Gallant on October 10 was referring to the elimination of *Hamas only*, not to the destruction of Gaza *as a society*. A better translation would be: "Gaza will not return to what it was before. *There will be no Hamas.* We will eliminate it all" (Rosenberg's emphasis). In response, the *New York Times* and the Associated Press both issued corrections, and this footnote is mine. "We will eliminate everything" is no longer a fair translation of Gallant's meaning. Still, "We will eliminate it all" is a fair summary—from the defense minister, no less—of the strategy the Israeli government eventually carried out. That true and correct statement can now have its rightful place among all the other true and correct statements of intent and incitement. I thank Rosenberg for his hard work making sure we all know exactly what the killers said.

Minister Bezalel Smotrich did the same with his appeal to "take down Gaza," as did National Security Minister Itamar Ben-Gvir when he described the whole Gazan population, guilty or otherwise, as "terrorists." As Malcolm Shaw, an international lawyer on the Israeli team, conceded, each of these men has the power to shape state policy and issue direct orders.[7] Yet Shaw characterized South African lawyer Tembeka Ngcukaitobi's thorough recitation of these quotes as "little beyond random assertions," insisting instead that these were rash statements pronounced in a moment of national trauma. Better, Shaw said, to give more weight to the panicked statements of exculpation made by Netanyahu and others in the week before the ICJ hearings.

(Not unrelatedly: Parties to ICJ disputes are allowed to appoint their own ad hoc judge to bulk up the usual fifteen-member panel. Israel nominated Aharon Barak, former president of the Supreme Court, who solemnly swore to exercise his powers "honorably, faithfully," and "impartially." On November 1, Barak stated, "I agree totally with what the government is doing." Square that circle.)[8]

Throughout the four-hour hearing, Israel's legal team referred again and again to Hamas, to its atrocities, and to its "genocidal" desire to end all Jewish life. This is the rhetorical crutch—a wind-up toy's mechanical catchphrase—for committed defenders of Israel's conduct in Gaza, and the early speeches looked more like a boisterous propaganda effort than a calm legal appeal. Yet the constant drawing of attention away from Israel's actions and toward those of Hamas also had a subtle legal function. At the core of Israel's arguments on Friday was a form of blackmail: a polite, legal, and deferential kind of blackmail, but blackmail nonetheless.

South Africa asked the court to rule that Israel should "immediately suspend its military operations in and against Gaza," in the hope that the mass killing of Palestinians might cease. Such a verdict, argued Christopher Staker, one of Israel's lawyers, would be an "irreparable prejudice to the rights of the respondent," meaning Israel's right to defend itself from attack. Because Hamas was not a party to the dispute between Israel and South Africa, it would not be bound by the court's judgment. If Israel were asked to stop bombing and Hamas were not, then by defending itself in any way Israel would be in immediate contravention of the court's ruling. Military action of any kind—genocidal or not—would be illegal. The nation would be, as Becker put it, "denied the ability to defend its citizens." The court, legally speaking anyway, is being held responsible for Israel's security.

Never mind that the real issue of substance is the methods Israel uses to "defend itself," not the right to self-defense as such: It is on this crucial point of rights that the ICJ's judgment will stand or fall. If the judges agree with Staker's subtle point and decline to call for a stop to the military campaign, the court will be denounced as morally bankrupt and utterly neutered by anyone who believes the Palestinians have their own right: a right to exist untroubled in the lands of their birth.

However humane and passionate and well reasoned the South African case, it contained a critical flaw. It failed to mention the simple fact of the ongoing war—this harsh, sanguinary war. And its omission meant that the Israeli lawyers were allowed to talk about nothing else. The South African team needn't have feared talking about the conflict: A genocide is still a genocide even if it takes place against

the backdrop of war. Indeed, this is the case in every clas-
sic example: the Armenian Genocide, Rwanda, Bosnia, the
Shoah. But in presenting their argument this way, the South
African lawyers showed themselves to be caught in the rhe-
torical trap that can so easily snare anyone who believes the
Convention is a faultless instrument of international justice.

The Convention—and the theory of genocide generally—corrupts our thinking about mass murder. To make
the case that a people are suffering or have suffered genocide, advocates and lawyers often have to warp the details
of the story so that the victims more closely resemble the
familiar archetype. In this instance, it is an ironic and
slightly grotesque distortion: To qualify as victims, to earn
international sympathy, Palestinians must appear to be just
as passive and just as innocent as the Jews once slain in the
Holocaust. Then again, bereft of a diplomatic patron and
legal linebacker like Israel has in the United States, these
are the tactics Palestinians have to resort to: cut out from
all other avenues of political pressure, such methods are not
first preferences but last resorts.

Thirty years ago, the regime of human rights and international law was hallowed as a salve and corrective for the
crimes of the recent past: a progressive vision of cold, hard
legal doctrine to tend swiftly to the victims of atrocity
anywhere, at any time. But thirty years of hypocrisy and
unpunished, uncondemned violations of that same law
and those same rights have delivered us breathless to this
moment of extreme precarity. The honor and esteem of the
court is at stake, and with it the whole value and worth of
international law.

CHAPTER SIX

IN THE DOCK, PART II
Matters of Permanence

New Republic, January 2024

In the dusk and dust of Gaza's ruin, the Israeli soldiers danced. "I'm coming to occupy Gaza/and beat Hezbollah," they chanted, "I stick by one mitzvah/to wipe off the seed of Amalek." It was December 7, two months after Hamas's attack on Israeli civilians. The troops formed a circle and continued their song: "I left home behind me/won't come back until victory/We know our slogan/there are no uninvolved civilians." The first refrain of their charming tune called back to Prime Minister Benjamin Netanyahu's evocation of the ur-enemy of the Jews; the final repeated line paraphrased their own head of state: "It is an entire nation out there that is responsible," Israeli President Isaac Herzog told the press in mid-October. "It is not true this rhetoric about civilians not being aware, not involved."[1]

Between an innocent Palestinian and a guilty one, Herzog saw no difference. Yoav Gallant, the defense minister, didn't either. When he ordered a siege of Gaza so total that "no electricity, no food, [and] no fuel" be allowed to enter, he decided that both guerilla and child alike should not survive the blockade. Israel Katz, now the foreign minister, likewise insisted that the "civilian population . . . will not receive a drop of water or a single battery until they leave the world." Palestinians cannot leave Gaza, so Katz presumably meant they would get nothing until they reached heaven, perhaps hell—either way, until they were dead. The dancing soldiers understood very clearly what was instructed of them. They followed a sacred commandment and joined in the vengeful chorus whose echoes can now be heard in the courtrooms of The Hague.

At the Peace Palace on Friday, the judges of the International Court of Justice took special care to quote these statements by Herzog, Gallant, and Katz.[2] The men's words, incriminating themselves as genocidaires as well as the state they serve, formed the backbone of the judges' ruling—a provisional, interim ruling—that there is a significant, plausible, prima facie threat of Gaza's Palestinians being destroyed "in whole or in part." The Israeli government and its army must, the Court ordered, "take all measures within its power to prevent the commission of [genocidal] acts." It must also "prevent and punish the direct and public incitement to commit genocide," an order that means that Netanyahu's government, if it cares at all about living up to the standards of international law it constantly trumpets, must immediately indict its own ministers and its own president.

South Africa, which brought the case before the ICJ, asked for nine provisional measures; the Court issued six, insisting that they "need not be identical to those requested." Still, the ruling rejected almost every objection—moral, technical, procedural—thrown up by the Israeli team in their messy appearance at the hearing earlier this month. The Court ruled that under the Genocide Convention, which binds all signatories to "prevent and punish" the crime, South Africa had solid grounding to bring a case; it also ruled that it had jurisdiction to issue measures and hear the full case later on. Importantly, and contrary to the Israeli defense team's best efforts, it recognized the right of Palestinians not to be subject to annihilation. In essence, Israel was read its Miranda rights: Any genocides you commit now can and will be later used against you in court. And there will be a later. A "preliminary objections" phase may follow down the line, in which the Israelis can challenge the Court's competence. For now, put bluntly, Israel is on trial for genocide.

To speak of "victory" for one side and "defeat" of the other, however, would be naïve and premature. The judges blankly refused to even mention South Africa's principal request: an immediate cessation of all military operations in Gaza. As morally outrageous as this refusal might seem, the judges were legally correct and followed the one coherent and sound objection made from the Israeli side. Any order rendering military action illegal would be binding on Israel but not Hamas, leaving the state unable to defend itself against attack; such a ruling would be prejudicial against a state's right to self-defense. And although South Africa asked for fact-finding teams to be allowed to enter Gaza, the Court requested only that Israel draw up a report on its compliance with the ICJ's order and refrain from destroying evidence.

Undeniably humiliating for Israel, however, were the voting margins. All of the Court's measures were accepted by a margin of 15–2 or 16–1. One judge—Julia Sebutinde of Uganda—voted against every measure on the grounds that the ICJ had no jurisdiction to hear the case, thus making her objection rather moot. Not even Aharon Barak, the former Israeli Supreme Court president appointed to the panel, went that far. Barak voted in favor of two of the Court's measures: the order demanding punishment for incitement, and the request for "immediate and effective measures to enable the provision of urgently needed basic services." Three months ago, Barak said he agreed "totally with what the [Israeli] government is doing," but perhaps he has since foreseen that his own legacy as a defender of his country's constitutional system is worth more than protecting Netanyahu before the judgment of the world.

On October 12, when Isaac Herzog gave his opinion that there was no difference between a Palestinian militant and a pregnant Palestinian woman, he was standing next to Ursula von der Leyen, head of the European Commission.[3] As Herzog spoke, von der Leyen blinked and said nothing. She heard it said, not a few inches from her own face, that an "entire nation" was guilty and deserving of death, and raised no objection. Western diplomats and politicians have done a lot of that recently: blinking and saying nothing, stirring only when the purse strings jingle and the Israelis ask for more ammunition. This is not a facetious observation: Most nations, including the United States, have strict rules against selling arms to nations that violate international law.[4] Though such a rule has not stopped gunrunners before, part of the worth of the ICJ's order is in having one more weapon that might be used to run a stick through the spokes of the machine, something that might, with a little effort, slow the tally of Palestinian dead from steadily ticking upward.

In delivering its statement just two weeks after hearing first submissions, the Court was clearly sensitive to the urgency of the Palestinian plight. Indeed, part of the task before the judges was to find whether South Africa's application was sufficiently urgent such that a ruling couldn't wait until later. (They found that it was.) For those Gazans still alive but on the edge of starvation, for those Palestinians sleeping now in the open and with no medical care at all, let alone power or potable water, the Court's speed matters. The Israeli government has now been told that it must give them aid and prevent their slow slide into oblivion. But what of the dead? What of the homes—360,000 of them, according to the ICJ—the IDF has shelled, bombed, and dynamited, to which no Palestinian can ever return?

The Israeli government insists its evacuation measures are only temporary. So was the Nakba. Perhaps as many as half of all Gazans have so far been permanently displaced. Permanence matters, because if the Israeli government chooses to ignore the Court's ruling and carries on its present course, then by the time the next stage of hearings begins, the Court will be asked to judge something that has already happened and has passed, with all its pain, into history. Even now, when a people might still be salvaged, permanent "solutions" are being suggested. Earlier this week, in a meeting with European diplomats, Israel Katz pitched building an artificial island off the Gazan coast. Clothing what he said in the benign language of "development," Katz didn't stop to ask whether it was his land (or sea) to build on, whether he had any right to it. This is what thinking looks like in the upper ranks of the Netanyahu war cabinet. Permanence is its goal, and no Palestinian—alive or dead—is allowed to object.

CHAPTER SEVEN

IN THE DOCK, PART III

Endgame in Rafah

New Republic, May 2024

They came to Rafah on a promise of safety: There will be no bombs here. You might even find a pinch of rice and some water for washing. So by ox cart and on foot, by pickup truck sagging under the load of a whole clan's belongings, a great mass of Palestinians moved through streets half-cleared of pulverized concrete, rubbish, and human shit, bound for what looked like a haven.[1] They came from Shujayya and Deir al Balah, from Gaza City and Nuseirat. Gazans interviewed by Doctors Without Borders speak of being pushed around as many as nine times, shuttled between the Strip's "evacuation zones," and converging, in the end, on the town at the furthest extremity available.[2] They came to Rafah, and after May 7, when the Israeli army announced its latest offensive into the town, they went. They were promised again that some-where else might be safe, but this time they embarked with less hope, fewer family at their side, their bellies emptier than before, carrying before them a scavenged scrap of white cloth to pass for a flag.[3] But even that will not grant them immu-nity from a blunt fact: At any moment, no matter what they are doing, they might be shot where they stand.[4]

For seven months, Rafah was the only place in Gaza resembling a functional society. It had a threadbare admin-istration, the last remains of an infrastructure, a few hospi-tals still running, and a border crossing used for the passage of aid. Its refugee population of one million (in peacetime it was home to a third of that number) was held in a state of sustained bare life. Now even that shall be stripped from them. On May 10, these facts compelled South Africa's law-yers to return to the International Court of Justice and try once more to get an order—a provisional measure—under the Genocide Convention to halt the onslaught.[5] The court has refused to grant South Africa's main request—a total and complete end to all Israeli military action in Gaza—three times. To ask again for a reconsideration, the South African lawyers have to demonstrate that the situation has significantly worsened. Their arguments at hearings on May 16 were consequently much more urgent and desperate than when they first appeared in court, in January. If the tone then was grave and dire, yesterday it was apocalyptic. The Rafah invasion, the lawyers argued, will be "the last step in the destruction of Gaza," the "endgame" for an entire people, the "last chance for the court to act."

As much as lawyers in wigs and robes can be when speak-ing to the highest court in the world, South Africa's advocates were abrupt and aggressive, clearly aiming to evoke in the judges a pang of complicity—a direct stake in lives that might yet be saved by their intervention. "Your previous orders have not succeeded in protecting" Palestinians, the lawyer Vaughan Lowe said bluntly. "Whether because [of] the lack of clarity as to precisely what the orders require or because Israel chooses to ignore them, they have not been effective." The judges should, Lowe continued, "spell it out explicitly for Israel" that the court is "not powerless" nor "worthless," consecrated alone "to assert not only its own authority but the authority of international law." Tembeka Ngcukaitobi reinforced this theme: "The rule of law can only survive through the orders of this court," he said. "If the rule of law is to have any meaning, let it be today and with this case."

The ICJ has shied from granting South Africa's principal plea for a complete withdrawal of Israel Defense Forces because it has been hemmed in by Israel's reasonable objection that any order issued against it would contravene its right to self-defense—especially given that Hamas (because it is not a state and not a party to the court) wouldn't be bound by the same order. It seemed, for a moment, that the South African team had found a sneaky and clever track around this barrier. The written submission for their latest plea for provisional measures included this formulation: Israel "shall immediately withdraw and cease its military offensive in the Rafah Governorate."[6] The request applied to Rafah alone; it would not extend to a similar prohibition in other parts of Gaza, allowing the judges much more room to condemn the latest offensive without breaching Israel's own rights. Though smaller in scale than previous requests, its effect would be wider.

By the time of the hearings on Thursday, however, that specific and finely honed wording was gone. At their conclusion, South Africa's lawyers demanded the IDF "immediately, totally, and unconditionally withdraw . . . from the entirety of the Gaza Strip." Quite why the South African side abandoned a finessing scalpel for the bludgeon force of a hammer is unclear. It closes off the space available to the judges to maneuver and presents them instead with a kind of ultimatum. But as the judges stated in their first decision on provisional measures, their opinion "need not be identical to those requested." The court can still issue a limited order that obliges Israel to withdraw from Rafah and reopen its border crossing, as well as the one at Kerem Shalom. It falls then to Israel to comply. The country's failure to do so would be an enormous detriment to its argument when, inevitably, some years down the line, we return again for the full case to be heard.

From late October last year, and every week since, Gazans have been given at best twenty-four hours to remove themselves from an area the Israeli army wishes to ruin. Yet when Israel's agents appeared before the ICJ on Friday, they complained loudly and at length that a few days was not time enough to summon its lawyers to The Hague. In contrast to the January hearings, their bench was empty; against South Africa's battery of six lawyers, Israel mustered only three. Just two spoke. Toward the end of their allotted time, someone in the gallery loudly shouted, "Liars!" Whoever they were, and as undignified as their outburst was, they were not entirely wrong.[7]

One chilling example stands out. After a two-week special forces operation against Al Shifa Hospital in April, the Israelis left behind a mass grave with thirty bodies inside, some with cannulas still in their arms.[8] Hundreds of other bodies were found around the hospital complex, including, if Hamas civil officials are to be believed, those of several doctors.[9] Yet Kaplan Tourgeman, a legal adviser in Israel's Foreign Affairs Ministry, stated: "Despite the intense military activity on the premises [of Al Shifa], no patients or medical staff were harmed during the operation by the IDF." Tourgeman's blatant lie also dodged overwhelming evidence of a similar mass grave of hundreds of bodies found near Nasser Hospital in Khan Younis, after a similar operation included among its remains corpses dressed in medical scrubs.[10]

Which is more crass? To fib about the pits your own soldiers likely dug or to accuse the other side of acting as an accessory to a terror group? Gilam Noam, Israel's deputy attorney general for international law, suggested South Africa's only motivation in coming to the court was to "obtain military advantage for its ally, Hamas, which it does not wish to see defeated." Noam claimed that the South African side's attempt to "exploit" the court was "vile and cynical" and that really it "wishes to see Hamas remain in control." Among the many high aims brought low by its conduct since October is the Israeli desire, as Noam put it, "to see a different future for Gaza." It will deliver that future at the point of a bayonet, and one cannot help but recall the prayer of a Buddhist activist in Vietnam at the beginning of America's bloody savaging of that country: "Lead us not into Salvation, but deliver us from Deliverance."[11]

It is tempting to regard the ICJ as merely a symbol. Impotent to intervene when it is needed most, it can appear to be an airtight realm in which reality and the law do not blend; anyone who stands accused by it can simply ignore its rulings. But its opinions do have an effect, if not the preferred one: A firm order from its judges would impose significant pressure on Israel's closest pals—the United States and Germany—to dam up the torrent of arms and ammunition they have unleashed to fuel Gaza's nightmare. Last week, the Biden administration delivered (to itself) an overdue report—in response to National Security Memorandum 20—which gave license (to itself) to continue these shipments, despite Biden's limp withholding of a few boats. The report found it "reasonable to assess" that American arms had been used in violations of international law in Gaza, yet because the study was not asked to judge the legality of each drop of a bomb or firing of a shell, or indeed to judge whether these things had happened at all, there was no real reason for the flow of arms to stop. The administration asked a foggy, bureaucratic question and got an equally foggy, bureaucratic answer back.[12]

A clear provisional measure from the ICJ would provide a legal standard the US (and other countries) would be obliged to follow. It would also give useful leverage to internal dissidents within governments to push harder for higher standards on arms transfers.* It might stop the grotesque daily ritual of officials appearing before the world

---

* Some officials in the US State Department, it seems, did try to slow down the shipment of arms. After stepping down as Israeli ambassador to the United States, Michael Herzog accused "bureaucrats" at State of repeatedly slowing down military aid: "There were [bureaucrats] who simply stopped these things, and there were legal officials who leaned very hard on the top brass of the State Department, including on secretary Blinken, not to authorize weapons transfers." (See "After finishing DC tour, an Israeli ambassador known for his discretion is ready to talk," *Times of Israel*, February 4, 2025)

and reassuring themselves (and us) that Israel complies always and forever with international law and any crimes that have occurred will be fairly investigated by the IDF. As a recent NPR report revealed, "Among the 1,260 complaints regarding Israeli soldiers harming Palestinians and their property" submitted to Israel's Military Advocate General's office between 2017 and 2021, "only 11 resulted in indictments—fewer than 1 percent of all complaints."[13] Actual prosecutions are so rare that the human rights group B'Tselem stopped contributing to them in 2016. Put simply, just as the state cannot be trusted to report on itself, it cannot be trusted to issue a verdict on itself either.

Anything could and should be thrown into the gears of the machine. Israel acts the way it does because of America's enduring role as chief armorer, banker, and patron. The Israeli air force does not load up its bombers without assurance that more munitions made by American hands are on their way; its politicians would not appear on a stage before a horde of settlers and promise them seaside homes on the Gazan waterfront if words like these weren't routinely defended by American politicians.[14] On whose behalf were American cops sent to smash the heads of American students? It was to the benefit of extreme-right Finance Minister Bezalel Smotrich, who, despite the ICJ's warning against incitement to genocide, is still calling for the "total annihilation" of Gaza.[15]

What does "total annihilation" look like? From the morass of suffering, examples and images tend to select themselves and lodge in the brain like an infection. Here is one. Sabreen Al Sakani lived in Rafah. She was thirty weeks pregnant. In April, she was killed in an Israeli airstrike, alongside her husband and daughter. Her body was taken to a hospital. Doctors performed an emergency caesarean outside, in the open air. The child was born, and her uncle called her Sabreen, after her mother. Sabreen survived for 120 hours.[16] A just world would reconsecrate itself in Sabreen's image, would title its legal codes in her name. Perhaps this is sentimental. Yet it is a better sentiment than the kind expressed by those who would call Sabreen's fate a "tragedy" rather than a crime. Codes are complex, yes; the law is a labyrinth; but justice is a smaller thing, and simpler too: It says no one should be born an orphan, dead in five days.

CHAPTER EIGHT

WITH HASTE TO THE HOLDING CELLS

The Question of British Complicity

New Statesman, **November 2024**

There have been many opportunities to confront Israel's cruelty in the past year. At every moment, the Western powers dodged their duty to protect the innocent and defend the legal order they claim to uphold. The issuing of arrest warrants for Prime Minister Benjamin Netanyahu and his former defense minister Yoav Gallant by the International Criminal Court (ICC) is a milestone both serious and seismic—and a challenge to that hypocrisy.[1] It means the political leaders of an alleged democracy cannot step foot in any of the 125 states—including Britain—that are party to the Rome Statute without risking arrest. It means they join Hamas commander Mohammed Deif (who is reportedly dead) on the list of individuals formally indicted for the kinds of offenses humanity has collectively agreed are gravest of all.[2] Yet today the British Home Secretary Yvette Cooper refused to say if she would arrest Netanyahu if he landed on British soil. Complicity with Israel's actions is no longer viable. Above all in the West, this warrant should mean that those nations which have up until now been happy to take Israeli money in exchange for weapons used for slaughter—the US, the UK, Germany—no longer have any legal justification to continue their deadly trade.

These countries could have acted earlier. They could have stopped in May, when the ICC's chief prosecutor Karim Khan (now under fire for alleged sexual impropriety) first recommended charges.[3] That same month the ICJ ordered an immediate stop to Israel's offensive in Rafah and a cessation of any act that might be genocidal. Who knows how many lives might have been saved in Gaza or Lebanon had they acted in July, when the ICJ also ruled that Israel's occupation of Palestinian lands was illegal?[4] The release of any of the damning, horrifying reports compiled by international bodies, civil society groups and human rights monitors should have been enough. The sight of nineteen-year-old Sha'ban al-Dalou being burned alive with an IV drip in his arm alone should have been enough.[5] Children crushed under ruins, children without heads, children in plastic bags: these, too, should have been enough.

The ICC's warrant also reveals the scale of Israeli methods. In Gaza, there is risk of famine.[6] Medical supplies necessary to treat the wounds inflicted by incessant airstrikes, artillery barrages, and sniper shots are precious and limited. Potable water ran dry long ago. When Yoav Gallant ordered on October 9, 2023, a siege so total "no electricity, no food, [and] no fuel" would be allowed to pass, he kept to his word. This statement, as in the ICJ rulings, forms the backbone of the ICC's argument proving intent.

Gallant and Netanyahu, the ICC alleges, "intentionally and knowingly deprived the civilian population in Gaza of objects indispensable to their survival." Such deprivation has "no clear military need or other justification. . . . Mr. Netanyahu and Mr. Gallant bear criminal responsibility for the war crime of starvation." Moreover, the ICC has enough conclusive evidence to allege more than just the criminality of a siege "calculated to bring about the destruction of part of the civilian population." As the ultimate heads of the Israeli armed forces, Netanyahu and Gallant are (or were) responsible for military actions and as such, the ICC states, bear "criminal responsibility as civilian superiors for the war crime of intentionally directing attacks against the civilian population."

In the year after 7 October, the Royal Air Force flew 645 reconnaissance flights over Gaza from their base in Akrotiri, Cyprus—more than the US and even Israel itself. Al Jazeera has alleged that these surveillance flights were also the source of targeting data provided to the IDF.[7] If this is the case, then the British government will have already passed from complicity to active involvement. The UK Ministry of Defence claims the RAF pilot orders are "narrowly defined" to "secure the release of the hostages only."[8]

When he was still in opposition, David Lammy said "all parties must uphold international law." Any breaches, he insisted, "should always be treated with utmost seriousness."[9] He did not act with utmost seriousness when he canceled only 30 of the 350 active British-Israeli arms export licenses in September.[10] That, too, was another missed opportunity, and another choice made to sacrifice the lives of Palestinians. It is a moral choice as much as much as it is a legal one, and there is only one answer. "We will not falter in our pursuit of peace," Keir Starmer proclaimed last month.[11] He has never failed to remind us that he was once a human rights lawyer. On his shoulders rests the responsibility to ensure that the cause to which he has allegedly committed his entire life— the cause of justice—will not be scoffed at by butchers. In doing so he must not become a butcher himself.

After the ICC's arrest warrants, anything less than an immediate and total British arms embargo on the state of Israel should be considered a plain endorsement of war crimes and crimes against humanity. Anything weaker than a blanket ban on the involvement of British military personnel and equipment in support of the IDF will transform abetment into active encouragement. If Keir Starmer and David Lammy—or any other Labour MP—wish to avoid imperiling their own souls or being tainted for the rest of their lives with the stink of the mass grave, they must sanction any sworn member of the Israeli government and the bloodthirsty settler movement it represents. The Home Office and the Attorney General ought to publicly commit themselves to a policy: if Benjamin Netanyahu or Yoav Gallant ever enter British territory they will face immediate arrest and the speedy transfer to a holding cell in The Hague.

If in the future there is to be any reckoning with the complicity of the British government in the annihilation of Palestinian life in Gaza, it is moments like these that will matter most, when political leaders can sense the evidence piling up and when they have both the political capacity and the moral will to act. The choice could not be starker: between direct collusion in a world-historic crime and the principled refusal to participate in an extermination.

CHAPTER NINE

THE TWILIGHT OF AMERICAN PRESTIGE

Joe Biden Is Trashing International Law

New Republic, **December 2024**

For once Matthew Miller, a man as sinister as he is bland, had nothing to say. It was unusual. Nearly every day of the last thirteen months has been witness to Miller's banal podium performances as spokesman of the State Department. Miller's role as mouthpiece: to run American complicity in the mass murder of Palestinians through the filter of colorless, exculpatory bureaucrat-speak.[1] Yet on November 21, mere hours after the International Criminal Court issued its warrants for the arrest of Benjamin Netanyahu and his former defense minister, Yoav Gallant, State abruptly canceled a scheduled press briefing.[2] There are, it appears, limits to Miller's powers of obfuscation. Words failed him. Just as words so often fail us when we face the scale of Gaza's destruction.

Silence too is an action, and the list of things the United States will not do to protect its accomplices is shrinking fast. The two highest courts in the world—the ICC and the International Court of Justice—now have open cases against the state of Israel and its current leadership. Rather than pull back a single inch, even to save its own face, the United States would prefer instead to trash these courts, the law they represent, and the moral principles they embody. Carry on like this, and the virtues America claims to defend will soon look exactly like what's left of Gaza: ruined.

This time it's personal. Netanyahu and Gallant stand accused of war crimes and crimes against humanity. As of last Thursday, neither man can visit any of the 125 nations party to the Rome Statute (including United Kingdom, Canada, and Germany) without serious fear of incarceration and speedy shipping to The Hague. They are marked men, branded as killers for the rest of their lives, confined to countries just as dismissive and offensive to international law as theirs is. These warrants are a monumental event. They prove two things: to lead an alleged democracy does not make you immune from justice, and for the Palestinians, as a people, there is hope yet that their assassins might suffer some punishment.

The warrants also reveal a world tipped sharply on its axis. The Nuremberg precedent, which serves as the foundation of modern international law, has always been thin and precarious—especially after Vietnam, after Iraq. The US acted in the postwar era as if the law was limp, placid, and pliable—a sidearm for the imperial hegemon rather than a gold standard applicable everywhere. But we scoff today to hear Secretary of State Antony Blinken trumpeting a "rules-based international order" precisely because that order has never been so openly insulted.[3] With one side of its face, the US smiles; with the other, it bites. The ICC was praised to high heaven when it indicted Vladimir Putin for his forced transfer of children from Ukraine. "I think," Blinken said in March last year, "anyone who's a party to the court and has obligations should fulfill their obligations."[4] Now, when the ICC applies the same standard toward an "ally," Joe Biden calls the court "outrageous."[5]

In one sense, the government of the United States—and its propagandists, like Matthew Miller—doesn't need to care. It is not a member of the ICC or a signatory to the Rome Treaty. Indeed, the US refused to join the court when it was formed twenty-two years ago, at the dawn of the "war on terror," to avoid moments like this. Senator Lindsey Graham admitted as much when he said, the US should "act forcefully against the ICC. . . . We cannot let the world believe for a moment that this is a legitimate exercise . . . because to do so means *we could be next*" (my emphasis).[6] Meanwhile, the American Service-Members' Protection Act is still in force, a law that allows the US to use "all means necessary . . . to bring about the release of any US or allied personnel being detained or imprisoned by, on behalf of, or at the request of the [ICC]." This law's nickname is The Hague Invasion Act.[7]

Intentional famine. Deliberate famine. Hunger as a weapon. These are Netanyahu and Gallant's crimes. The pair, according to the ICC, "intentionally and knowingly deprived the civilian population in Gaza of objects indispensable to their survival." As such, they bear "criminal responsibility for the war crime of starvation." And these are crimes still ongoing. Blinken gave Israel thirty days to improve the grotesque humanitarian strife in Gaza or face "implications for US policy."[8] He gave no clue of what those "implications" might be. That was on October 13. The Israel Defense Forces allowed a few more aid trucks to enter. Not nearly enough to improve Palestinian life above the condition of bare, meager existence. But it was enough for the US to admit, thirty days later, that those threatened "implications" no longer mattered. It was another "red line" to be passed over at the same speed as the "red line" drawn before the Rafah offensive in May—an offensive the ICJ insisted should cease immediately.[9]

On October 9 last year, Gallant incriminated himself with the infamous "No electricity, no food, no fuel" order. Today's dire circumstances are no different. That instruction still stands. Indeed, to apply any caveats whatsoever on aid entering Gaza's ruins is a violation of Israel's legal duty. The ICC noticed the country's duplicity here, stating that deliveries "were not made to fulfil Israel's obligations. . . .They were a response to the pressure of the international community or requests by the United States." Regardless, that aid was "not sufficient." Gaza remains held in a sick stasis. Every soul is suspended, kept alive long enough for the cold to kill them this Christmas. Or disease. Or dumb bombs made by American hands.

Netanyahu and Gallant face arrest for these strikes as well, these "widespread and systematic" attacks. The ICC indicts them with "criminal responsibility as civilian superiors for the war crime of intentionally directing attacks against the civilian population." This alone proves the Israeli army and its intelligence agencies are incapable of prosecuting the war in a manner that even begrudgingly allows for the right of Palestinians to live. Israel's defenders, including the US, would protest that Netanyahu's regime is engaged in a conflict against valid enemies. Regardless of the battle against Hamas or Hezbollah, they have, by their methods, forfeited the right to pursue the war on their own terms.

Like its client and customer, the US finds itself at the opposite end to the goal of greater justice. Daily it sacrifices the postwar legal and moral order on the altar of Israeli arrogance and bloodlust. It is to Netanyahu and Gallant's benefit that Joe Biden destroys whatever respect the rest of the world might still have for one of the proud authors of Nuremberg. And as Biden passes into political senescence, retiring shamed to his wintry Delaware home, we should hope that his mental agility is not as far decayed as it looks. Because only those sound of mind are able to reflect on a lonely legacy: The adamantine support Biden offered, as the representative of totemic American power, on the side of two men indicted for the acts humanity has collectively judged to be gravest of all. Short of joining the pair in the dock as a coconspirator, we can wish too that late at night he weeps the tears of the guilty. The twilight of his life and presidency is the twilight of American prestige.

CHAPTER TEN

THE INTELLECTUALS LOSE THEIR MINDS

Howard Jacobson's Folly

The Dreadnought, **December 2023**

We get by most days ducking uncomfortable facts. The train's late again. Your boss is a tyrant. The country's run by crooks. A dozen eggs cost half a day's paycheck. Too much newspaper space that ought to be reserved for the thoughtful and smart is occupied by the clueless and stupid. Better to grumble and gripe than paralyze yourself with worry about stuff like this. But there are moments that oblige our attention, times to heed what we otherwise defer.

We live in such a moment now. Conscripted witnesses to a clerically psychopathic Israeli government staffed by settler-zealots wielding the justification of a savage atrocity to carry through a far larger atrocity in the hope of securing their final wish: a state that really does run from the Jordan to the Mediterranean and which, when complete, will call the messiah to waft down and land his dainty blessed feet on the piled-up skulls of an eviscerated Palestinian nation. In hope we turn to the intellectuals to clarify and inform on our behalf, who can attack the criminal and murderous and defend the defenseless in language better and more meaningful than we can. The newspaper writer's responsibility here is doubled because their words might make a difference to a party platform or encourage an anxious mind to protest. Instead, we find them behaving like drooling and swampish ghouls.

Look at the way the comic novelist Howard Jacobson mewled and slurred and slandered his way through a column in Sunday's *Observer*.[1] I single out Jacobson not for the sake of it (and certainly not for the fun of it) but to hold him up as an exemplar of the register a number of famous intellectuals now write in, a tone of voice somehow weepy, stroppy, self-pitying, and paranoid as well as embarrassingly bombastic and bloodthirsty. What unites them around Jacobson's style and theme also drives their rage: fewer and fewer people are willing to give their blanket consent to the Israeli state and forgive everything it does. Lashed by this knowledge—which can never be publicly admitted— they've stooped to fighting harder and dirtier than ever, contorting themselves into undefendable positions, and are going mad in the process.

Deadbolting himself inside the mental hothouse of his own making, Jacobson's crankery blushes and blooms like an obscure and precious flower.* "Among the casualties of

---

*   Mark the sequel. Another Jacobson derangement (*The Observer*, October 6, 2024) tried to argue that broadcasters like the BBC showing footage of maimed and wounded children in Gaza—as

(Continued)

this war," he declares, "are the young." True enough. Though Jacobson isn't referring to the 6,000 children slain since the siege and invasion of Gaza started, nor the many hundreds whose uncounted bodies rest putrefying in the rubble the Israelis have so expertly made, nor the many hundreds of thousands more shorn from their homes and the succor of their parents. Jacobson isn't even referring to the Israeli children still yet cruelly held ransom in the Strip. The target of his spittle, the true object of his fury, is the impressionable youth of Western university campuses who, under the snake-eyed sway of their professors' "lurid language," are engaged in a "scurrilous and orchestrated" campaign to mock and offend Jewish suffering.

Their chosen method for mocking Jewish suffering is to point out that Israel's conduct in Gaza is approaching (or has already surpassed in thought and deed) the threshold of genocide. Morality changed after October 7th, Jacobson claims: "Black became white, evil good, ugliness beauty, the victim the culprit." It's open season on the Jews, apparently. The best method to humiliate them is to charge them with the same crime to which they were once subjected. The "sensationalist pronouncements" of genocide, he says, emulsifying his metaphors better than Julia Child mixes a cake batter, do no more than "flutter like so many pennants at a medieval joust" yet are also the words which "go off like hand grenades." Either way, another crime is in progress,

---

is their public duty—was really a kind of blood libel. To simply air the fact of Israeli actions was, according to Jacobson, a kind of anti-Semitism, "dipping into the communal pile of prejudice and superstition. . . . Here we were again, the same merciless infanticides inscribed in the imaginations of medieval Christians."

a crime far worse in Jacobson's eyes than the systematic destruction of a doubly oppressed people—that of throwing the Holocaust back in the teeth of the Jews:

> There is a sadistic triumphalism in charging Jews with genocide, as though those making it feel they have their man at last. The sadism resides, specifically, in attacking Jews where their memories of pain are keenest. By making them now the torturer and not the tortured, their assailants wrest their anguish from them, not only stealing their past but trampling on it.

As it happens, I'm extremely doubtful "genocide" is the most useful method to condemn the continued sacrifice of Palestinian lives and am prepared to defend my view against any comrade who wishes to challenge it—or against any enemy who would interpret my doubt as an exoneration of Israeli actions. Howard Jacobson also knows quite a lot about the Shoah; he treats it seriously, more seriously than most, and I've quoted him approvingly in the past when he insulted those who would cheapen or sentimentalize the midnight of the century.[2] But what makes his performance in the *Observer* so galling, so outrageous—what makes him more extreme even than Simon Sebag Montefiore, Hadley Freeman, Zoe Strimpel, or that twinky quisling and charity-bin Powellite Douglas Murray[3]—is his construction and defense of a standard that can never be met; a standard which, had anyone else invented it, would be harshly condemned as supremacist blackmail. Jacobson has found the means to argue—argue poorly, but argue nonetheless—that "the Jews" can never commit a crime against humanity;

indeed, can never be accused of committing one. Not now, not in 2018, 2014, 1982, or 1948, but *never and for all time.*

"Brutality," he neatly intones, "is not genocide." Perhaps not, but what is? The lonely bit of evidence Jacobson offers for believing the IDF is innocent of an exterminatory design is the army's use of handbills dropped on their prisoners. "Genocides don't leaflet the populations they want to destroy," he says. Mentioning the leaflets (or the text messages) is a commonplace plea, held up by those who would prefer to use international law as a piece of clay molded and stretched to create the gaps a bomber pilot can fly through. Forewarning is an essential part of the modern "humane" method of terror-bombing, giving legal cover to the killer and passing the fault to the victim for failing to move out from the blast radius. In another sense, the leaflets are part of the psychological operation of terror. Those impossible notices, dropped from the sky, predict a future—a future of murder. *Here is our warning, we can do much worse,* they seem to say. *This could be a bomb, for now it's only paper.*

Later in his slumping effort, Jacobson mentions Dostoyevsky as the novelist who best understood the "perverse exhilaration of impiety" on the part of the Jew-haters (these Jew-haters who he neither names nor identifies). But Dostoyevsky also wrote about the unendurable torture of knowing the date and time of your own death. No sane person desires to learn for certain that their life is forfeit; better to embrace death than trust in its promise. From *The Idiot*:

> the worst, most violent pain lies not in injuries, but in the fact that you know for certain that within the

space of an hour, then ten minutes, then half a minute, then now, right at this moment—your soul will fly out of your body. . . . When you put your head right under the guillotine and hear it sliding above your head, it's that quarter of a second that's most terrible of all. . . . Who can say that human nature is able to endure such a thing without going mad? . . . No, a human being should not be treated like that . . .[4]

This is the present condition of every soul in Gaza, simultaneously suspended and threatened, and it is the broken psyche the world bears responsibility for mending once the destruction ends. But notice the path the leaflets have taken. First in the north, forcing Gazans to flee south; then in early December they were dropped in the south, where Gazans fled to—and now where are they to go? Herein lies the trap set for them, which Howard Jacobson agrees is "brutal" but not criminal—indeed, *can never be criminal*. They cannot leave because they are Palestinians. This is their territory, no matter how squalid and miserable and lorded over by a psychopathic social and political order. They cannot leave because the Rafah gate will not be opened, and if it did, the expulsion of the larger part of the population would be demanded. In fact, is being demanded, in the plan being shipped around for the moral and financial assent of American lawmakers. How much closer must the IDF get to the enactment of a great historical crime before Howard Jacobson, and everyone who shares his slipping grasp on reality, finally dissents?

Having hacked through the dense thicket of mock-religious invocation and cleared out the underbrush of literary allusion, you can't help but notice—miles-wide and yawning—the void where his citations and sources ought to be. If there really are "leftist intellectuals who have the hots for terrorists," as he claimed in another performance, then shouldn't he name names?[5] The hysteric who thinks with the blood, who believes the ethnos binds all and always, is never far from the McCarthyite impulse. Yet Jacobson cannot turn informer, cannot emulate the yellow model of the rat, cannot hot-dial the Prevent program, because there is nobody of any note who believes any of the things he's attributed to them. Why such imprecision and vagueness? Why turn cowardly at the exact moment when his rage is hottest? Because, at root, Jacobson and others like him are having this argument with other Jews.

Oh, how they wish it weren't the case. How they yearn to magic that fact away. How much simpler it would be for them to endlessly shift responsibility onto a faceless and morbid mob of students. It's certainly an easier target than someone who shares the same experience, knows what pride is at stake, and has a better sense of when someone is wasting their own worth. When Jews demand an end not only to the present campaign of sadism but the continued illegal occupation of Palestinian lands in general, they are speaking not against their own history and faith but through those trials and because of those lessons. It cannot escape Jacobson's attention that the two intellectuals who have done more than anyone to expand and popularize the use of the term genocide—Omer Bartov and Raz Segal— are both Israelis. Surely, he must have clocked that in the front ranks of every demonstration and protest since the start of the nightmare, arm in arm with Palestinians, have been movements like Jewish Voice for Peace (in the US) and Na'amod (in Britain). These radicals are certainly smarter than Jacobson—braver, too—and possess a better under-standing of the slogan "Never Again" than he does. Either that cry is an appeal to universal principles, or it is reserved for a single ethnicity alone; either mass murder is forbidden everywhere or never.

The sublimation of this fact—the fiercest critics of Israeli policy and the policy of its armorers are Jews as well—and its diversion into a mythical mob at which he can wag a scolding finger leads Jacobson into the sallow caves of falsehood; he can't even get his history right. "Calling Zionist Jews Nazis," he says, "was an early go at discrediting them, inversely, by equating them with their murderers." (Again, who is doing the "calling"?) Being rude to Zionists is about as Jewish a tradition as Hanukkah, and it began long before the Nazis ever troubled the scene. The socialists and internationalists of the Bund saw early the inner damage a narrow national-ism would inflict, and it was Henryk Ehrlich (son-in-law of Simon Dubnow, no less) who correctly identified Herzl and Nordau's extreme utopia as representing "the interests of capitalism, national chauvinism and clericalism . . .

Have then the Zionists, with their insane plans for transforming the small Jewish minority in Palestine into a majority . . . not stirred up with their own hands the fire of Arabian and Moslem fanaticism? Was it not only anti-democratic and reactionary, but almost mad and absurd to support Jewish coloniza-tion by the power of British bayonets instead of by an honorable understanding with the Arabs?[6]

Ehrlich and his comrades also observed and were outraged by the miserable alliances Zionists had to enter to carry through their "mad" and "absurd" ambition, shaking hands with the same people who thought *Yes, the Jews really should live elsewhere.* The Zionists didn't want them in Poland, in Ukraine, or in Hungary any more than the fascists did, and when they adopted "Jews to Palestine" as a slogan and practice they spoke in harmony with the same people who, just a few years later, put them all in pits. Ehrlich was not without cause when he said Zionism, as a movement and a goal, "should consider anti-Semitism as a blessing, because Zionism is nurtured by anti-Semitism. Likewise, Zionism is a precious good for the anti-Semites."[7] This morbid dynamic still festers today in the fascist camp where pound-shop Mosleys yearn for Israel's expansion so that it might have room for the rest of Europe's Jews, and in megachurch pulpits where Ben-Gvirist attitudes are celebrated as a necessary prelude to the apocalypse.

There is a beautiful and ironic dream which lives in the seed of Palestinian liberation. It is a dual liberation: the end of the Occupation means not only salvaging Palestinian existence but ending the need for depraved alliances between enemies; it means doing away with the debauched mentality that obliges people like Howard Jacobson to behave less decently than they would to anyone else. The war always returns home. The system of barbed wire, machine-gun nests, and torture chambers brutalizes its victims and corrupts equally the perpetrators and those who would guard them from any accusation. "How long have you been in the claws of the tank?" the poet Mahmoud Darwish once asked. Much, much too long.

CHAPTER ELEVEN

THE ANNIHILATION PLAN

The Settlers Make Their Move

New Republic, December 2024

Twenty-five shekels for a T-shirt declaring "Gaza is part of the Land of Israel." Ten for a phone case. Fifty shekels for a forty-eight-piece jigsaw puzzle of a territory being cleaved apart. Also for sale: baby onesies branded "Yishai," the name of a settler camp planned for the ruins of Beit Hanoun, a town in northern Gaza, in case you want to dress your child in the uniform of a movement cheering the murder of several thousand other children.

It was Sukkot, the Jewish festival, not far from kibbutz Be'eri, on the eastern side of the border fence. Israel's powerful messianist cause had convened a conference called "Preparing to Settle Gaza"—the sequel to a jubilant convention held in Jerusalem last January.[1] As kids played safely in the sand, a ring of bored soldiers slumped in white plastic chairs guarded the camp and several members of Israel's legislature. Punctuating the speeches was the low periodic thud of artillery, a crackling ripple of demolition charges, and, if you listened closely, the italic whistle of bombs. A few miles away: the entrance to the Netzarim Corridor—the three-mile-wide zone bisecting the Strip, built by the Israeli army to enable its continued clearance of the land.[2]

The settler movement's plans to reconquer the Strip and build on the ruins of Palestinian lives align neatly with those of the state that is today clearing the desired real estate. What was a crude dream in early 2024 is now, as the year comes to an end, being made with bulldozers and blasting caps a cruder reality. South of Netzarim there is starvation, disease, occasional airstrikes, and above all a sense of suspension—stasis, waiting.[3] North of Netzarim, the army is snapping tight its noose. Everything above Gaza City is a free-fire zone.[4] The operation there is the blueprint for what will follow again in the south, in the center, and everywhere else until the land and its people are no more.

There is a word, better than the ubiquitous genocide, to distill the monstrous totality of what is underway in the north of Gaza, and the clarity of the mission: *extermination*. And this rampage might be the first example of a modern war where its butchers tell you what they're doing while they're doing it. "What is happening there?" asks Moshe Ya'alon, former chief of the Israel Defense Forces, referring to Gaza's northernmost towns. The army is "essentially cleansing the area of Arabs."[5] Starting in early October, the enclave was sealed.[6] No aid allowed in, only people allowed out. Not for the first time were Palestinians, some 200,000 of them, commanded to leave. Their exodus—to where? No place is safe—became a death march, as they were exposed above to the bomber pilots and operators of drones; Salah al Din Road was and is a shooting gallery.[7] Into November the air campaign thumped on. Hospitals were blasted repeatedly.[8] Individual strikes killed twenty, thirty, eighty people at a time.[9] On October 29, in the suburb of Beit Lahia, bombs flattened a five-story apartment block, burying under it ninety-three Palestinians.[10] Perhaps as many as 75,000 people remain in this closing circle. Every last one of them, according to the Israeli army, is a fair target.

"It's permissible and even recommended to starve an enemy to death," according to Giora Eiland, ex-head of Israel's National Security Council. "The only ones who will be left in that area will be terrorists who will surrender or die of starvation."[11] Eiland is one of the authors of the now-notorious "Generals' Plan," a ruthless strategy put forward in September by a group of retired military officers frustrated that Hamas fighters keep reappearing in places thought to be cleared. Its methods are simple: Isolate an area, amputate the aid, then squeeze. While Eiland might complain within earshot of Benjamin Netanyahu that his schemes have not been formally adopted, the plan's spirit pervades the army.[12] A better name for it might be the "Hunger Plan"; the "Annihilation Plan." In Eiland's judgment, it is only the beginning. "Israel's government sees the ability to win in northern Gaza as a first stage that will lead to a permanent Israeli military government," Eiland explained. "In the next stage maybe also to renewed settlement."

Eiland likes to pose as a hardened paratrooper: a no-bullshit blusterer, ignorant of political chicanery, who is merely applying cold analytical logic to a military problem. But his problem—Israel's problem—is not military alone. An occupying power is obliged to preserve the lives of the people under its control, to give them aid, to not dynamite their homes. But Eiland sees no distinction between citizen and combatant. He does not discriminate. "The people of Gaza are like the people of Nazi Germany," the general has said. He means the people are complicit. He means they are guilty. He means they deserve to die—an attitude that runs through the entire upper rank of the Israeli government. "North Gaza is more beautiful than ever," claims Amichai Eliyahu, the heritage minister. "Blowing up and flattening everything is beautiful." To the troops, the ex–defense boss Yoav Gallant says, "We are fighting human animals, and we are acting accordingly." And the troops reply: "There are no uninvolved civilians."

Netzarim is the puncture wound in Gaza's side. It drives westward from the border with Israel, where those settlers had their exultant meeting, to the Mediterranean. Along this freshly paved road: checkpoints, army camps, supply dumps, surveillance posts, buffer zones, sewage piping, electricity wires, cell towers, kitchens, prefab synagogues.[13] To make way for all this superb infrastructure, these foundations on which the settlers can later build, everything else—the homes, the shops, the bakeries, the masjids, the museums—must be removed. "There was not a single construction left that was taller than my waist anywhere except our bases and observation towers," one soldier told *The Guardian*.[14] IDF squads have been so busy they keep running out of explosives. Similarly, back in the north, Israeli construction firms deeply connected to the nexus of land clearance and settlement building in the West Bank are being given contracts to carry out demolitions.[15] "I think," Avi Dichter says contentedly, "that we are going to stay in Gaza for a long time." Avi Dichter is the minister for "food security."

We all know the old cliché about the first casualty in war being truth. The powerful and their propagandists need not be smart creatures, only talented—in the same way a serial killer is talented. Talent in making black appear white, a grim picture rosy, a cruel policy necessary. War requires a skill for euphemism of the kind Netanyahu displayed when he said back in January that "Israel has no intention of permanently occupying Gaza or displacing its civilian population."[16] After Human Rights Watch, in a long mid-November report, starkly accused the Israeli government of causing the "mass and forced displacement of the majority of the civilian population . . . a widespread and systematic" policy that amounts to a "crime against humanity,"[17] the Israeli foreign ministry's spokesperson Oren Marmorstein replied, "Israel's efforts are directed solely at dismantling Hamas's terror capabilities."[18] Sometimes the fables are so blatant you do not know whether to laugh bitterly or shiver.

Yet, for every hard question dodged and every accusation smoothed over, there is someone like Eiland or Dichter to state the obvious. And what is the obvious? What are they doing? Gaza is the zone where the super technological is used to inflict a primitive form of life on an undeserving mass. A bare life. This is the latest frontier of elegantly computerized mass killing: a new way to carry out an old sin. The prestige of their machines is at stake: AI and algorithms, night-piercing radar, mass surveillance, the avionics of an F-35 jet. Can the killing be done fast enough? Trillions of dollars spent to design, build, arm, and operate a fleet of devices so that for every mother killed in Gaza, six children die with her—in her apartment, in her tent, on their street.[19] The gleam of military might deployed for the vaporizing of families waving white flags and bearing all their worldly goods on their backs.

Here, on the waterfront, we see—many of us for the first time at real scale—what total power freed from any self-restraint—the limits of the law, and the outrage of the world—is capable of doing. This is what any regime can do to anyone perceived to be mounting a challenge to its authority. Daily that power proves its intent: to maim and dispossess and destroy without discrimination. The many thousands still trapped in the north of Gaza have taken the only decision left available to them: to choose where they die. Like Ahmed, from Beit Lahia. "There's nowhere else to sleep or pitch a tent, or even to find a tent," he told the Israeli newspaper *Haaretz*. "It's a fact that people aren't streaming out of the area, as happened at the beginning of the war, because from their standpoint, no place is safe anymore. It would be better to die near home and to take comfort in dying in the area where we've been living."[20] Defiance *of* death is not a choice on offer. But you can be defiant *in* death. This too is a kind of resistance, a symbol of humanity, the spit in the eye of those who treat them as unhuman.

CHAPTER TWELVE

NOT THE END, MAYBE THE BEGINNING

A Ceasefire, at Last

New Republic, January 2025

For the first time in thirteen months, a hush will fall over Gaza. Starting Sunday and for the next six weeks at least, soccer fans, sweet-sellers, and students will not be obliterated at random and for no reason. In return for this moment's quiet, thirty-three Israeli hostages—women, the infirm—will be exchanged for several hundred Palestinian prisoners. And if that quiet holds for longer than six weeks, with a little negotiation, the remaining male hostages might see light again, released with the bodies of those slain in captivity.[1]

Palestinians cheered in Deir al Balah last night. They flew their colors in Khan Younis. Anas al-Sharif, a reporter for Al Jazeera, announced news of the ceasefire on camera while steadily removing his blue helmet and "press"-stamped flak jacket. He was lifted on the shoulders of a small crowd.[2] At least 165 journalists have been murdered in Gaza—part of the 46,000 people who have been killed that we know of so far.* Part of the 110,000 who have been maimed. One hundred people a day for 467 days.[3]

Yesterday's announcement of a ceasefire between Israel and Hamas—achieved under American pressure—was necessary, urgent, and overdue.[4] So is the tempered relief that comes with it. There will be time now to find the dead; perhaps even the months necessary to mourn them. But a pause is not peace. Stasis is not an end. It is in the nature of occupations that they lead to bloodshed. For so long as Israel clings to land that is not its own and covets more, murder will recur with the certainty of the seasons. A ceasefire is only the first step, the barest minimum, in righting this historic offense to justice.

---

*   A comprehensive analysis published in *The Lancet* spanning October 2023 to the end of June 2024 concludes that the official death toll from traumatic injury is undercounted by 41 percent. Extrapolating from June to October 2024 suggests the number of violent deaths in Gaza exceeds 70,000, though this number does not include non-trauma deaths, for example by starvation or disease. Another analysis in *The Lancet* applied the ratio of direct to indirect deaths in historical conflicts and suggested the total toll caused by the war could be as high as 186,000. (See Zeina Jamaluddine, Hanan Abukmail, Sarah Aly, Oona M. R. Campbell, Francesco Checchi, "Traumatic injury mortality in the Gaza Strip from Oct 7, 2023, to June 30, 2024: A capture–recapture analysis," *The Lancet* 405, no. 10477, February 8, 2025, 469–477; Rasha Khatiba, Martin McKee, Salim Yusuf, "Counting the dead in Gaza: difficult but essential," *The Lancet* 404, no. 10449, July 20, 2024).

The agreement itself is nervous and provisional. It describes probationary periods, talks about talks, while leaving the stickiest and most serious issues, such as who shall govern the blighted Strip and what control the Israeli army will exert, still not addressed in full. And even at this eleventh hour—as it squeezes in as many late bombing runs as it can—the Israeli government is threatening to collapse the deal, just as it has done previously when any hint of a break in the fighting looked near.[5]

During these six weeks, the forced evacuation orders in place on the Strip will fall away; Gazans are free to return to their homes. Though to talk of "freedom" and "homes" seems absurd in this light. It is easier, when reporting of Gaza's dismemberment, to mention what remains rather than to list what is done and gone forever.[6] What is there? Rubble, mostly. Under that rubble, corpses not included in official tolls. A lot of people stricken in the mind and the body. The roads remain, yes, insofar as routes have been cleared through the dust of what used to be familiar streets. Who will do the mending? The usual confluence of over-stretched aid groups, volunteer nurses, émigré teachers. Not Israel, no. Not the United States, although both should bear the burden of repair, for they together made this wreckage. Instead, the Palestinians of Gaza—Palestinians in general, subaltern peoples everywhere—shall be made to remember that they have been *disciplined*. That extermination, even if its perpetrators have stepped back from the brink this time, was *possible*.

The Israeli army shall remain just inside the border fence. The buffer zone that the troops will continue to occupy is seven hundred meters deep. But there is no mention yet of what shall become of the Netzarim corridor, the militarized belt that cleaves Gaza in half from its easternmost border to the Mediterranean. However, an occupying power does not spend massive resources on elaborate infrastructure—checkpoints, camps, surveillance posts, cell towers, synagogues—for land they do not covet and do not, at some point soon, hope to permanently settle.

With this ceasefire secured, Benjamin Netanyahu can show up in Poland in a week's time for the eightieth anniversary of the liberation of Auschwitz-Birkenau. Many European countries, including Germany and the UK, have collectively (if covertly) decided that arrest warrants issued by the International Criminal Court are optional, unnecessary for their professed commitment to global justice.[7]

Indeed, Netanyahu can make his appearance at the last major occasion when survivors of the Shoah will be well and able enough to attend. There he can say his solemn and statesman-ish things, with little awareness of just how yawning a hole he has punched in the moral, legal, and political fabric of the postwar world. This world, made on the ruins of Auschwitz itself, is the same one invoked by Netanyahu in defense of this inhuman war in Gaza. "All these universalist reference points—the Shoah as the measure of all crimes, antisemitism as the most lethal form of bigotry—are in danger of disappearing as the Israeli military massacres and starves Palestinians," the intellectual Pankaj Mishra wrote in his landmark essay, "The Shoah after Gaza": "Netanyahu and his cohort threaten the basis of the global order that was rebuilt after the revelation of Nazi crimes."[8]

With or without a halt in the fighting, there is going to be a genocide trial at the International Court of Justice. It might take years to get to that point, but the state of Israel will be in the dock. Unlike the ICC process, it does not require Netanyahu and ex–defense chief Yoav Gallant to be present, however satisfying that might be. This process, like the mending of Palestinian minds and bodies, is just as urgent as any ceasefire, or whisper of a new peace process, for it will establish a new kind of Nuremberg precedent— the governing rule for a reality after Gaza's ruin.

Meanwhile, Gaza itself will remain a frozen graveyard, a place where the few outlets for Palestinian despair will either be exile, suicide, or martyrdom in the ranks of a Hamas rebuilt with the spoils of rage. The party has potent symbols with which to recruit and rebuild, among them its former leader Yahya Sinwar's last acts of defiance, fiercely fighting the occupiers. Brutalization, hardening, coarsening: These too are potent instruments for the renewal of the conflict. And they run both ways, afflicting perpetrator and victim alike. A legion of Israeli soldiers will return to their families and think of their time in this zone where anything was allowed.[9] And perhaps they will consider how much of their own behavior reminds them of their most notorious enemies.

This is only a pause for another breath. It can only be a pause for breath. The knife is still in the hand.

GENOCIDE ON TRIAL
Meaning and Moral Failure

New Republic, November 2023

Just days after Hamas unleashed its death squads to behead kibbutzniks with shovels, and Israel, with a quick clench of an already tightened fist, began its total siege and terror-bombing of Gaza, the Israeli academic Raz Segal sounded an early warning. Deprived of the essentials of life and denied the possibility of escape, the captive Palestinians of Gaza face a "textbook case of genocide." Israel's "genocidal assault," Segal wrote in *Jewish Currents*, is "explicit, open, and unashamed."[1] In the month since Segal's article, his indictment and prophecy have been taken up as the principal cry of those who demand an immediate end to all hostilities.

At rallies and sit-ins and demonstrations and in countless open letters and polemics, the specter of genocide has been evoked as a forbidding sanction against the elimination of Palestinian life. Some eight hundred scholars of human rights (including leading figures like the Israeli historian Omer Bartov and the Turkish historian Taner Akçam) warned in mid-October that an "illegal, potentially geno-cidal siege" was leading "to an outright destructive assault."[2] In a furious final letter to his boss before retiring, Craig Mokhiber, the director of the New York office of the UN High Commissioner for Human Rights, quoted Segal's accusation of "a genocide unfolding before our eyes."[3] A week and a half ago, three Palestinian human rights orga-nizations filed suit with the International Criminal Court, alleging genocide alongside war crimes and crimes against humanity.[4] The aptness and power of the word is reinforced by its absence in the mouths of politicians, who, whether out of cowardice or conviction, refuse to indict their own governments with complicity in the ultimate crime.

Language often turns limp in the face of atrocity. Confronted with a vast catastrophe, we reach for something that can sum up the cruelty of the present. What term is more culturally potent than genocide? By December 1948, when it was adopted by the General Assembly of the United Nations, the Genocide Convention, an international treaty that forbids any "intent to destroy . . . a national, ethnic, racial, or religious group," was already embedded in the tapestry of international law as a self-evident good beyond contest.[5] In its concatenation of Greek and Latin, the term itself seems to come to us from deep within the bowels of antiquity. Other crimes—even those proscribed during the Nuremberg trials of leading Nazis by the Allies—sit in the shadow of genocide, and we speak of it with a solemn frown, reverent of its gravity. Genocide is a kind of negative

sublime, the ballast by which all other human wrongdoing is measured: something not of this earth, the gravest of
deeds, the crime of all crimes.

Of course, it is precisely those ideas that seem obvious
and self-evident that deserve to be questioned. It is even
more important to do so when they are invoked as a talis-
man of justice in moments of profound crisis. Look a little
closer and it becomes apparent that genocide is a flawed
idea, a compromised theory whose hollow clauses don't
support its moral weight and lead us no closer to justice.
The term is somehow too narrow and too ambiguous; its
definition is too strict and too indistinct. As a piece of law,
the Genocide Convention excuses and exonerates more perpetrators of mass murder than it condemns. It is so full of
holes that academics have spent the last seventy-five years
confecting new interpretations to make it work.[6] Genocide
is supposed to be a crime so total and unimaginable that
only a few other events are allowed to join the Holocaust
as the preeminent exemplar of human evil; in this way, it
leaves out all the other mass slaughters for which the twentieth century is so notorious. What if, as the historian Dirk
Moses, author of *The Problems of Genocide*, has suggested,
"the house of international criminal law was built on shaky
conceptual foundations"? What if genocide "is a part of the
problem of civilian destruction rather than its solution"?[7]

It was a fluke that the term ever entered the world, and
a kind of accident that it became the most serious statute
on the lawbooks of civilization. Having endured an arduous
voyage to the United States from Poland, and though not an
international lawyer, Raphael Lemkin's 1944 book *Axis Rule
in Occupied Europe* sought to fill in what he perceived as a

gap in the rules governing the behavior of states. His definition of his own coinage was sweeping: "A coordinated plan of different actions aiming at the destruction of essential foundations of the life of national groups."[8] He imagined an arsenal of techniques that could lead to the ruin of a group: denial of self-government, attacks on its intelligentsia, bans on native language, educational indoctrination, economic exploitation, manipulation of birth rates, and the destruction of a group's culture (its art, memorials, religious sites, libraries). Mass murder—the physical destruction of a group—was only the most extreme form, and it was entirely possible, Lemkin reasoned, for genocide to take place without anyone ever being killed.

Though he would later try to cover up his personal convictions in an attempt to present himself as an impartial avatar of human justice, Lemkin's stress on national and ethnic groups was drawn from his decades of experience as a passionate and dedicated member of the Zionist movement.[9] His most basic ideas about nationhood and civilization, his belief in what he mysteriously called the "biological structure" of a potential Jewish nation, and his belief in the eternal problem of anti-Semitism were formed out of his Zionism and fed directly into his conception of genocide as the end result of a kind of irrational atavism: an apolitical crime of prejudice or, as Dirk Moses semi-sarcastically puts it, a "massive hate crime."[10] But nations aren't "biological" entities—they are social and cultural formations resting on a shared mythology of unity and belonging.[11] Religions don't have a "biological" element either; in fact, a religion would be pretty useless if it denied itself converts and stuck to an ethnic or "racial" basis. From the start, Lemkin conceived of genocide as an exclusive and ethnic crime—not the total and overarching wrong we believe in today.

Lemkin's book arrived too late to be considered seriously by the Allied prosecutors building their case for the forthcoming trials at Nuremberg. Even when they heard about his idea, they were skeptical, even outright scornful. The British team especially thought the term was "too fancy" and "outlandish" and "couldn't understand what the word meant."[12] Regardless, the Allies already had their trifecta of crimes that would be the anchor of accountability in the postwar era: war crimes, crimes against peace, and crimes against humanity. Of these, the waging of aggressive war was deemed the most severe. "To initiate a war of aggression," the Nuremberg judges wrote, "is not only an international crime; it is the supreme international crime differing only from other war crimes in that it contains within itself the accumulated evil of the whole."[13] No Nazi was ever convicted of genocide at Nuremberg; no Nazi was ever charged with genocide.

Here, with Lemkin's snubbing by the Allies, the story of genocide might have ended: not in defeat, but in dismissal. It could have been just another chapter in just another academic monograph. Except Lemkin, humiliated and embarrassed, never forgave the snub. He described the handing down of the Nuremberg verdicts as "the blackest day of my life"—a peculiar and solipsistic view on a historic moment for international law, and on a judgment that convicted the killers of much of Lemkin's family.[14] Lemkin's righteous revenge was to dodge the Nuremberg precedent by appealing to the UN General Assembly and the world's press. He left his law career to remodel himself as an activist and amateur diplomat, writing indignant letters to anyone with authority, even buttonholing statesmen in the Delegates Lounge of the UN.

As Lemkin's theory found favor with the assembly (especially countries emerging from under the colonial heel) and made its way through the grinder of resolutions, consultations, debates, secretarial drafts, and committee hearings, it was pruned and reshaped into something else. A consensus hardened: Rather than a broad chain of actions and techniques, genocide now described the physical destruction of a group alone. What emerged after eighteen months of squabbling, in December 1948, was a stripped-down and strict interpretation of Lemkin's original concept.[15] The Convention had been gutted of everything that made genocide a unique idea, particularly Lemkin's notion of cultural genocide (or "vandalism," as he called it). In this narrower conception of the term, all the artistic, intellectual, and spiritual achievements of a group—indeed, their very history—could be erased and, so long as their bodies were left untouched, such acts would not count as genocide.

Raphael Lemkin went along with the remaking of his idea because he had shackled himself so completely to its success. The Convention had to be ratified no matter the cost to his own intellectual integrity or the thoroughness of his theory. And the costs were high. In his ceaseless lobbying, Lemkin removed "political groups" from Convention drafts, thereby restricting the pool of victims to national, ethnic, religious, and "racial" groups. The consequences were immediate: It was now possible to annihilate a political movement without committing genocide, a fact that proved helpful for the US-backed Suharto regime in Indonesia when it purged and destroyed one million "Communists"; for Mao's Cultural Revolution in its purge of the "filth" of the "reactionaries"; for the regimes of torture and disappearance in Latin America. The definition worked retroactively too, letting the British off the hook for their murderous colonial police actions, and the Soviets for their elimination of the prosperous peasants they called "kulaks." Moreover, the most outrageous kinds of ethnic violence could be excused if the killers claimed the justification of political repression, as with Operation Searchlight in 1971, when the Pakistani army tried to brutally put down Bangladeshi demands for freedom and self-determination. Not only were political groups excluded, other minorities were refused the protection of the Convention as well. During the war, the Nazis had pursued sexual minorities and the disabled with equal cruelty to Jews, Roma, Slavs, and Communists, but that fact did not conform neatly to Lemkin's national, ethnic, or religious guidelines.[16]

Some of the faults embedded in the idea of genocide were Lemkin's own; some were the result of his capitulation to the powerful. Britain, the United States, and the Soviets worked hard to make sure the Genocide Convention (or the Nuremberg precedent, for that matter) would not halt the remaking of the world after World War II—what Samuel Moyn has called the "brutal peace."[17] Two doctrines had to be rescued from the Convention's weak snares: military necessity and population transfer. In the postwar order, people would have to conform to borders rather than borders to people. As the UN debated Lemkin's idea, millions of ethnic Germans were forced out of Eastern Europe, the partition (and parturition) of India and Pakistan caused one of the largest mass migrations in human history, and Israel carried out its takeover of Palestine at the expense of its non-Jewish inhabitants. The complete dispossession and immiseration of an enormous number of people was the sin the large powers (and plenty of smaller nations) swallowed in order to secure the postwar settlement. When "mass displacement of populations" was taken out of the draft Convention under the excuse that it "did not necessarily mean the physical destruction of a group," the UN created a yawning loophole in the crime of genocide.[18]

The Allies also made sure their vast arsenals, their fleets of bombers, and their new atomic weapons could be used on civilians without consequence: The justifications of military necessity and national security would cleanse all sins. "Killing masses of civilians," Moses writes, "was not illegal if motivated by military goals: victory, not destruction."[19] In a total war, an entire nation can be crippled by bombs and fire, its environment poisoned, millions of its non-combatants can be slain, to such a degree that it imperils the nation's existence, yet so long as the perpetrator uses that grotesque euphemism "collateral damage," there is no genocide. No death toll can appeal against it. Viewed this way, the notorious, muddled, misleading phrase "intent to destroy" begins to look a lot like a get-out clause or an escape hatch for the powerful. Built into the Convention is a seed of its own negation, a critical flaw that works to the benefit of the murderer—just enough cloudiness and imprecision that doubt can easily be thrown on any accusation of genocide. The centerpiece of international law, its strongest supposed pillar, should not be so patchy.

A hierarchy of crimes is not necessarily a bad thing. We know instinctively that murder is a graver act than theft or fraud, so why shouldn't mass murder be considered graver still?[20] The trouble is that this particular hierarchy of international law, which places genocide above all other crimes, has led to a perverse situation where it becomes ever easier for elites to pursue criminal policies—covert wars, occupations, economic sanctions and blockades, environmental spoliation, population transfers, secret funding of death squads—when they can claim a justification that does not reach the apex of that hierarchy. The belief in genocide as the preeminent crime shadows all those other bits of international law that do prohibit these actions, and in the process makes them less important and less accessible to everyday language. Worse still, we would be outraged if the crime of homicide said that some groups of people cannot be victims.

However, there is an alternative concept: crimes against humanity, which encompass any "systematic attack" on civilians, including mass murder, apartheid, sexual violence, and political persecution.[21] By a strange quirk of history, the inventor of that term, Hersch Lauterpacht, was a Zionist in interwar Poland like Lemkin. They went to the same law school in Lviv, and both had the same essential insight about the need for a single piece of international law to protect civilians. But Lauterpacht's idea has none of the knots and hang-ups that Lemkin's does. It is a universal concept rather than an ethnically specific one; it is neat and elegant and can be applied to different kinds of violence—not just physical destruction. Like so many other crucial parts of international law, the charge of crimes against humanity has been overshadowed and pushed aside by genocide. Then again, the idea contains in its name the very thing that is defied when anyone violates it: humanity.

Lauterpacht never needed to water down his theory. Lemkin, on the other hand, was more than happy to pare back his idea in order to see it enshrined in law. His colleagues were astonished that he was "willing to throw anything and everything overboard in order to save a ship."[22] If you wanted to be sympathetic to Raphael Lemkin, you would say that his fate was tragic. But tragedy implies thwarted innocence. Until his death in 1959, Lemkin went about his gutting of genocide willingly, single-mindedly pursuing his objective of ratification until eventually he found himself at rock bottom: as an anti-Communist-for-hire, getting into public disputes with the early leaders of the Civil Rights struggle and actively denying the severity of white supremacy in the United States.[23] When Lemkin was campaigning for the ratification of his Convention, he compromised his idea so often and so completely for the benefit of the powerful that he left us clutching a neutered piece of law that does little but protect the unjust.

ACKNOWLEDGMENTS

Supreme and enduring thanks are due to Emily Cooke of the *New Republic*, whose consistent discernment, flair, judgment, and principle were vital to the strength of the journalism collected here. Every month for more than a year, Emily helped to refine my flabby outrage into sharp and streamlined arguments. And to have had a small part in turning the magazine away from its historic blunders on Palestine is an emblem of pride I will wear for a long time.

Dirk Moses is a scholar of immense brilliance and composure, without whose insights, learning, and moral force this work would be much poorer. My thanks also to John Merrick, Jacob Abolafia, Grigor Atanesian, Mohammed Mhawish, Catherine Percival, Kate Bugos, and Megan Gibson.

For moving at immense speed while protecting the moral core of this book, Stephan Zguta is a champion editor deserving of all plaudits. For keeping the faith, for being fine company with exquisite taste, and for grasping the urgency of the moment as an agent, Michael Mungiello has earned my undying gratitude.

My first book was dedicated to my mother. This one is too. Courage, conviction, and compassion are but a handful of the many examples she has set. I can only hope to one day live up to them. I repeat with a full and blazing heart:

With her, anything is possible.

NOTES

Preface: While Looking Heaven in the Eye

1   "Smotrich 'assured' Israel would continue war and take control of Gaza," *Middle East Eye*, January 18, 2025, https://www.middleeasteye.net/news/smotrich -received-assurances-israel-continue-war-take-control -gaza.

2   Sarah El Deeb, "The war in Gaza has wiped out entire Palestinian families. AP documents 60 who lost dozens or more," Associated Press, June 17, 2024, https://ap news.com/article/gaza-palestinians-families-israel-war -deaths-a9f8bcfe402c17f1f78903eae67b7a7d.

3   Malak A Tantesh, "'My memories are crushed and buried': a long walk home in Gaza," *The Guardian*, January 31, 2025, https://www.theguardian.com/world /2025/jan/31/memories-crushed-buried-long-walk -home-gaza.

4   Rebecca West, "Greenhouse with Cyclamens I (1946)," in *A Train of Powder* (Ivan R. Dee, 1955), 10.

5   Margherita Stancati, Abeer Ayyoub, "In Gaza, Authorities Lose Count of the Dead," *The Wall Street Journal*, April

28, 2024, https://www.wsj.com/world/middle-east/in
-gaza-authorities-lose-count-of-the-dead-779ff694.

6   Jonathan Masters, Will Merrow, "U.S. Aid to Israel in
     Four Charts," Council on Foreign Relations, November
     13, 2024; Linda J. Bilmes, William D. Hartung,
     Stephen Semler, "United States Spending on Israel's
     Military Operations and Related U.S. Operations in
     the Region, October 7, 2023—September 30, 2024,"
     Watson Institute for International and Public Affairs,
     October 7, 2024.

7   "The UN Mine Action Service (UNMAS) has warned
     that between 5 to 10 percent of weapons fired into Gaza
     have failed to detonate": "Aid efforts in Gaza escalate, as
     risk from deadly unexploded ordnance grows," United
     Nations, January 29, 2025; Abubaker Abed, "Explosive
     Remnants in Gaza Cause Dozens of Casualties," *Drop
     Site*, February 13, 2025, https://www.dropsitenews
     .com/p/unexploded-ordnance-gaza-munitions.

8   Quoted with the gracious permission of the writer.
     Mohammed R Mhawish, "Snapshots: I spoke with 20
     people in Gaza after the ceasefire. My heart broke 20
     times," February 5, 2025, https://www.mohammed
     mhawish.com/p/snapshots-i-spoke-with-20-people.

9   By far the best single collation of references over the
     course of the war has been Lee Mordechai's "Bearing
     Witness to the Israel-Gaza War," available in English
     and Hebrew at https://witnessing-the-gaza-war.com/.

10   Aimé Césaire, *Discourse on Colonialism* (Monthly Review
     Press, 2000), 36–41.

11 Saul Friedländer, *Diary of a Crisis: Israel in Turmoil* (Verso, 2024), 6.

12 Ronen Bergman, Adam Goldman, "Israel Knew Hamas's Attack Plan More than a Year Ago," *The New York Times*, November 30, 2023, https://www.nytimes.com/2023/11/30/world/middleeast/israel-hamas-attack-intelligence.html.

13 Friedländer, *Diary of a Crisis*, 101.

14 Herzog gave this answer to British channel ITV's international correspondent Rageh Omaar during a press conference in early October. See Rageh Omaar, "Israeli president Isaac Herzog says Gazans could have risen up to fight 'evil' Hamas," ITV News, October 13, 2023, https://www.itv.com/news/2023–10-13/israeli-president-says-gazans-could-have-risen-up-to-fight-hamas.

15 Gallant made these remarks during a military briefing. See Emanuel Fabian, "Defense minister announces 'complete siege' of Gaza: No power, food or fuel," *Times of Israel*, October 9, 2023, https://www.timesofisrael.com/liveblog_entry/defense-minister-announces-complete-siege-of-gaza-no-power-food-or-fuel/.

16 Far from hiding Ben-Gvir's incitement, these remarks (made on Channel 12, November 11, 2023) were clipped and uploaded to his Jewish Power party's YouTube channel: https://www.youtube.com/watch?v=2yRl-cc-D3w.

17 Israel Katz (@Israel_katz), "We have to draw a line," https://x.com/Israel_katz/status/1712876230762967222.

18   Avi Dichter, appearing on Channel 12, November 11, 2023, see Hanno Hauenstein (@hahuenstein), https://x .com/hahauenstein/status/1723441134221869453.

19   Nissim Vaturi (@nissimv), "Now putting all disagree-ments aside," October 7, 2023, https://x.com/nissimv/ status/1710694866009596169; Vaturi was later part of the mob that broke into Sde Teiman torture facil-ity *in defense of the guards' right to rape Palestinian pris-oners*, see Emanuel Fabian, "'Bordering on anarchy': IDF chief sounds alarm after right-wing mob overruns 2nd base," *Times of Israel*, July 30, 2024, https://www .timesofisrael.com/bordering-on-anarchy-idf-chief -sounds-alarm-after-right-wing-mob-overruns-2nd -base/.

20   Noa Shpigel, "Israel's Far-right Minister Smotrich Calls for 'No Half Measures' in the 'Total Annihilation' of Gaza," *Haaretz*, April 30, 2024, https://www .haaretz.com/israel-news/2024–04-30/ty-article/. premium/smotrich-calls-for-no-half-measures-in-the -total-annihilation-of-gaza/0000018f-2f4c-d9c3-abcf -7f7d25460000.

21   Accompanied with a video of an IDF bulldozer on a rampage: Amichai Eliyahu (eliyau.a), Facebook, November 1, 2023, https://www.facebook.com/eliyau .a/videos/148918588283326.

22   Adam Taylor, "With strikes targeting rockets and tun-nels, the Israeli tactic of 'mowing the grass' returns to Gaza," *The Washington Post*, May 14, 2021, https: //www.washingtonpost.com/world/2021/05/14/israel

-gaza-history/; see also Gideon Levy, *The Punishment of Gaza* (Verso, 2010).

23 "On Oct. 27, three weeks into Israel's punishing counter-attack in Gaza, top Biden officials privately told a small group assembled at the White House what they would not say in public: Israel was regularly bombing buildings without solid intelligence that they were legitimate military targets." See Yasmeen Abutaleb, John Hudson, "How Biden became embroiled in a Gaza conflict with no end in sight," *The Washington Post*, March 18, 2024, https://www.washingtonpost.com/politics/2024/03/18/biden-israel-gaza-rafah-palestinians/

24 Emanuel Fabian, "Gallant: Israeli moving to full offense, Gaza will never return to what it was," *Times of Israel*, October 10, 2023, https://www.timesofisrael.com/liveblog_entry/gallant-israel-moving-to-full-offense-gaza-will-never-return-to-what-it-was/.

25 "The assessment, compiled by the Office of the Director of National Intelligence and described to CNN by three sources who have seen it, says that about 40–45% of the 29,000 air-to-ground munitions Israel has used have been unguided." See Natasha Bertrand, Katie Bo Lillis, "Nearly half of the Israeli munitions dropped on Gaza are imprecise 'dumb bombs,' US intelligence assessment finds," CNN, December 14, 2023, https://edition.cnn.com/2023/12/13/politics/intelligence-assessment-dumb-bombs-israel-gaza/index.html.

26 Estelle Shirbon, Pola Grzanka, "Israeli soldiers play with Gaza women's underwear in online posts,"

Reuters, March 28, 2024, https://www.reuters.com /world/middle-east/israeli-soldiers-play-with-gaza -womens-underwear-online-posts-2024–03-28/; Nina Berman, "Violating Intimacies," *Mondoweiss*, February 29, 2024, https://mondoweiss.net/2024/02 /violating-intimacies/.

27   "'The Mosquito Procedure is fully institutionalized, and it's a very gray area within the army,' a Nahal Brigade soldier said, explaining that the army tries to cover it up by shifting blame to junior soldiers. 'It's something that comes down as an explicit order from the battalion commander level and below. But some-where at the brigade commander level, they com-pletely deny it. When problems start, they push the responsibility downward and say not to do it.'" See Illy Pe'ery, "Israeli soldiers used an 80-year-old Gazan as a human shield. Then they killed him," *+972 Magazine*, February 16, 2025, https://www.972mag.com/gaza -human-shield-mosquito/.

28   Tom Stevenson, "Rubble from Bone," *London Review of Books*, February 8, 2024.

29   "In the fifty-six years since it occupied the Strip in 1967, Israel has transformed Gaza from a territory politically and economically integrated with Israel and the West Bank into an isolated enclave, from a func-tional economy to a dysfunctional one, from a pro-ductive society to an impoverished one." See Sara Roy, "The Long War on Gaza," *New York Review of Books*, December 19, 2023.

30 "Israeli Forces' Conduct in Gaza," Human Rights Watch and Oxfam Submission to Biden Administration's NSM-20 Process, March 19, 2024.

31 Alex de Waal, "How to Measure a Famine," *London Review of Books*, February 6, 2025.

32 Loveday Morris, "Far-right Israeli settlers step up attacks on aid trucks bound for Gaza," *The Washington Post*, May 26, 2024, https://www.washingtonpost .com/world/2024/05/26/west-bank-aid-trucks-gaza -settlers/; Lorenzo Tondo, Quique Kierszenbaum, "Israeli soldiers and police tipping off groups that attack Gaza aid trucks," *The Guardian*, May 21, 2024, https: //www.theguardian.com/world/article/2024/may/21 /israeli-soldiers-and-police-tipping-off-groups-that -attack-gaza-aid-trucks.

33 Jeet Heer, "How Biden's Foreign Policy Destroyed His Presidency," *The Nation*, January 17, 2025, https://www .thenation.com/article/world/biden-gaza-legacy -foreign-policy/.

34 Oliver Browning, "Israeli tank drives over 'I love Gaza' sign as military takes control of Rafah crossing," *The Independent*, May 7, 2024, https://www.independent .co.uk/news/israel-war-hamas-gaza-rafah-invasion -b2540856.html.

35 United Nations Office for the Coordination of Humanitarian Affairs, Humanitarian Situation Update #263, February 11, 2025.

36 "A needs assessment, carried out by a Gaza-based NGO sponsored by the War Child Alliance charity, also found that 92% of the children in the survey were 'not accepting of reality,' 79% suffer from nightmares and 73% exhibit symptoms of aggression." See Julian Borger, "Death feels imminent for 96% of children in Gaza, study finds," *The Guardian*, December 11, 2024, https://www.theguardian.com/world/2024/dec/11/death-feels-imminent-for-96-of-children-in-gaza-study-finds.

37 Willem Marx, Jerome Socolovsky, Kat Lonsdorf, Michele Kelemen, Greg Myre, James Hider, "Israel and Hamas reach a Gaza ceasefire agreement," NPR, January 15, 2025, https://www.npr.org/2025/01/15/g-s1–42883/ceasefire-israel-hamas-gaza-hostage-release.

38 William A. Schabas, *The Trial of the Kaiser* (Oxford University Press, 2018).

39 Ernest Hemingway, *The Sun Also Rises* (Random House, 1930), 141.

40 Vladimir Nabokov, *Pnin*, (Vintage, 1989), 120.

41 Emine Sinmaz, "'I'm so scared, please come': Hind Rajab, five, found dead in Gaza 12 days after cry for help," *The Observer*, February 10, 2024, https://www.theguardian.com/world/2024/feb/10/im-so-scared-please-come-hind-rajab-six-found-dead-in-gaza-12-days-after-cry-for-help; "The Killing of Hind Rajab," *Forensic Architecture*, June 21, 2024.

42 I. F. Stone, "People Without a Country," from *In a Time of Torment* (Jonathan Cape, 1968), 156.

43 Itamar Mann, "Farewell to the Rules-Based Order," *Verfassungsblog*, November 8, 2024, https://verfassungs blog.de/farewell-to-the-rules-based-order/.

44 David Rieff, *Slaughterhouse: Bosnia and the Failure of the West* (Touchstone, 1995), 9–10.

Introduction: A Missed Moral Lesson

1 I. F. Stone, "The Harder Battle and the Nobler Victory," *In a Time of Torment* (Jonathan Cape, 1968), 441–444.

2 Yaniz Roznai, Rosalind Dixon, David E Landau, "Judicial Reform or Abusive Constitutionalism in Israel," *Israel Law Review* 56, Special Issue 3: The Constitutional Crisis in Israel, November 2023, 292–304.

3 Christopher Hitchens used to call up Israel Shahak, for a long time the chairman for the Israeli League for Human and Civil Rights, and ask his opinion on events. Shahak would reply: "There are some encouraging signs of polarization."

4 Jacob Abolafia, "Lucid Dreamers," *The Point*, March 30, 2023, https://thepointmag.com/forms-of-life/lucid -dreamers/.

5 Ash Obel, "Police minister: Jews must go to Temple Mount on Passover—but no animal sacrifice," *Times of Israel*, April 3, 2023, https://www.timesofisrael.com /police-minister-jews-must-go-to-temple-mount-on -passover-but-no-animal-sacrifice/.

6   David Gritten, Yaroslav Lukov, "Al-Aqsa mosque: Violence as Israeli police raid Jerusalem holy site," BBC, April 5, 2023, https://www.bbc.com/news/world -middle-east-65184207.

7   The judgment of Benny Morris, Israel's most promi-nent historian and the epitome of a liberal Zionist: "Israel, certainly for the moment, can be consid-ered the least safe place on earth for Jews." Benny Morris, "Israel's Security Depends on Rafah," *New York Times*, April 11, 2024, https://www.nytimes.com /2024/04/11/opinion/israel-hamas-rafah-gaza.html.

8   Netanyahu's strategy in May 2024, as in February 2025, was to make deliberate provocations to Hamas so as to force a response. Qassam Muaddi, "Netanyahu's latest strategy to avoid a ceasefire, explained," *Mondoweiss*, August 21, 2024, https://mondoweiss.net/2024/08 /netanyahus-latest-strategy-to-avoid-a-ceasefire-explained/.

9   Darwish wrote this line with Muin Bseiso, whose son protected the poets' papers during this war. It reso-nates with Brecht's War Primer: "General, your tank is a powerful vehicle. . . . But it has one defect/It needs a driver." Esmat Elhalaby, "Our Siege is Long," Public Books, October 27, 2023, https://www.publicbooks. org/our-siege-is-long/.

10   I. F. Stone, "What It's Like to Be in Saigon," *In a Time of Torment* (Jonathan Cape, 1968), 272.

11   Henriette Chacar, Ali Sawafta, "Netanyahu's post-war plan says Israel to keep security control on Palestinian areas," Reuters, February 23, 2024, https://www.reuters

.com/world/middle-east/israels-netanyahu-presents
-first-official-post-gaza-war-plan-2024–02-23/.

12 James Robins, "The Israeli Settler Movement's Ugly
    Postwar Plans for Gazal," *New Republic*, February 19,
    2024, https://newrepublic.com/article/179087/israeli
    -settler-movement-ugly-postwar-plans-gaza/.

13 "Israel's Smotrich urges 'complete destruction' of Gaza
    instead of truce talks," *Middle East Eye*, April 26, 2024,
    https://www.middleeasteye.net/news/israel-far-right
    -minister-calls-complete-destruction-gaza.

14 Netanyahu denies saying this, of course. Raoul
    Wootliff, "PM rebuts claim by Rabin's granddaughter
    that his aide cast ex-PM as 'traitor,'" *Times of Israel*,
    October 21, 2018, https://www.timesofisrael.com/pm
    -rebuts-claim-by-rabins-granddaughter-that-his-aide
    -cast-ex-pm-as-traitor/.

Chapter One: Scour the Earth

1   Joseph Heller, *The Stern Gang: Ideology, Politics, and
    Terror, 1940–1949* (Routledge, 1995), 115; see also
    Heller, "The Zionist Right and National Liberation:
    From Jabotinsky to Avraham Stern" in Wistrich &
    Ohana, *The Shaping of Israeli Identity: Myth, Memory,
    and Trauma* (Routledge 2013).

2   Ofer Aderet, "Zionist Militia's Efforts to Recruit
    Nazis in Fight Against British Are Revealed," *Haaretz*,
    June 21, 2023, https://www.haaretz.com/israel-news
    /2023–06-21/ty-article-magazine/.highlight/zionist
    -military-org-efforts-to-recruit-nazis-in-fight-against

-the-british-are-revealed/00000188-d93a-d5fc-ab9d
-db7ae0ea0000.

3   "2 Ex-Stern Gang Members Admit Murdering U.N.
     Aide," *Los Angeles Times*, September 11, 1988; see also
     Christopher Hitchens, "Minority Report," *The Nation*,
     August 7/14, 1989, 159.

4   Christopher Hitchens, "Holy Land Heretic" in *Prepared
     for the Worst* (Chatto & Windus, 1988), 335–336.

5   Elias Feroz, "Thirty years after Baruch Goldstein's mas-
     sacre, his followers are now carrying out a genocide,"
     Mondoweiss, February 27, 2024, https://mondoweiss
     .net/2024/02/thirty-years-after-baruch-goldsteins
     -massacre-his-followers-are-now-carrying-out-a-genocide/.

6   "War of Independence veteran, 95, volunteers to join
     IDF in fight against Hamas," *The Jewish Chronicle*,
     October 12, 2023, https://www.thejc.com/news/war
     -of-independence-veteran-95-volunteers-to-join-idf
     -in-fight-against-hamas-sgh6h8cv.

7   Ofer Aderet, "Testimonies From the Censored Deir
     Yassin Massacre: 'They Piled Bodies and Burned
     Them,'" *Haaretz*, July 16, 2017, https://www.haaretz
     .com/israel-news/2017–07-16/ty-article-magazine
     /testimonies-from-the-censored-massacre-at-deir
     -yassin/0000017f-e364-d38f-a57f-e77689930000.

8   Statement by PM Netanyahu, Office of the Prime
     Minister of Israel, October 28, 2023.

9   Ryan Grim, Prem Thakker, "Biden's Conspiracy Theory
     About Gaza Casualty Numbers Unravels upon Inspection,"

The Intercept, October 31, 2023, https://theintercept
.com/2023/10/31/gaza-death-palestine-health
-ministry/.

10 Jacob Abolafia, "Lucid Dreamers," *The Point*, March
30, 2023, https://thepointmag.com/forms-of-life/lucid
-dreamers/.

11 Jonathan D. Strum, "The symbiotic relationship
between Netanyahu and Hamas," *The Hill*, October 10,
2023, https://thehill.com/opinion/international/4268794
-the-symbiotic-relationship-between-netanyahu-and
-hamas/.

12 Dmitry Shumsky, "Why Did Netanyahu Want to
Strengthen Hamas?," *Haaretz*, October 11, 2023,
https://www.haaretz.com/israel-news/2023–10-11/ty
-article/.premium/netanyahu-needed-a-strong-hamas
/0000018b-1e9f-d47b-a7fb-bfdfd8f30000.

13 Amaney A. Jamal, Michael Robbins, "What Palestinians
Really Think of Hamas," *Foreign Affairs*, October 25, 2023,
https://www.foreignaffairs.com/israel/what-palestinians
-really-think-hamas.

14 Max Saltman, "As Azerbaijan claims final victory in
Nagorno Karabakh, arms trade with Israel comes under
scrutiny," CNN, October 4, 2023, https://edition.cnn
.com/2023/10/04/middleeast/azerbaijan-israel-weapons
-mime-intl/index.html.

15 Yuval Abraham, "Expel all Palestinians from Gaza,
recommends Israeli gov't ministry," *+972 Magazine*,
October 30, 2023, https://www.972mag.com/intelligence
-ministry-gaza-population-transfer/.

Chapter Two: Even If the People Perish

1   Laila Hussein Moustafa, "When libraries like Gaza's are destroyed, what's lost is far more than books," *Los Angeles Times*, December 12, 2023, https://www.latimes.com /opinion/story/2023–12-12/gaza-library-bombing.

2   Dan Sheehan, "Israel has damaged or destroyed at least 13 libraries in Gaza," *Literary Hub*, February 6, 2024, https://lithub.com/israel-has-damaged-or-destroyed -at-least-13-libraries-in-gaza/.

3   "Israeli Damage to Archives, Libraries, and Museums in Gaza, October 2023–January 2024," Preliminary report from Librarians and Archivists with Palestine, available at https://librarianswithpalestine.org/gaza-report -2024/.

4   Sarvy Geranpayeh, "Gaza City archives among heritage sites destroyed in Israel-Hamas war," *The Art Newspaper*, December 22, 2023, https://www.theartnewspaper .com/2023/12/22/gaza-city-archives-among-heritage -sites-destroyed-in-israel-hamas-war.

5   Ibtisam Mahdi, "The obliteration of Gaza's multi-civilizational treasures," *+972 Magazine*, February 17, 2024, https://www.972mag.com/the-obliteration-of-gazas -multi-civilizational-treasures/.

6   "Gaza's Palace of Justice courthouse demolished 'by IDF' as new footage leaked," Sky News, December 5, 2023, https://news.sky.com/story/gazas-palace-of -justice-courthouse-demolished-by-idf-as-new-footage -leaked-13023501.

7   Mohamad El Chamaa, "Gazans mourn loss of their libraries: Cultural beacons and communal spaces," *The Washington Post*, December 1, 2023, https://www .washingtonpost.com/world/2023/11/30/gaza -library-palestinian-culture/.

8   Stephennie Mulder, "Gaza's oldest mosque, destroyed in an airstrike, was once a temple to Philistine and Roman gods, a Byzantine and Catholic church, and had engravings of Jewish ritual objects," *The Conversation*, January 17, 2024, https://theconversation.com/gazas -oldest-mosque-destroyed-in-an-airstrike-was-once -a-temple-to-philistine-and-roman-gods-a-byzantine -and-catholic-church-and-had-engravings-of-jewish -ritual-objects-220203.

9   Kaamil Ahmed, "'Everything beautiful has been destroyed': Palestinians mourn a city in tatters," *The Observer*, February 4, 2024, https://www.theguardian .com/world/2024/feb/04/everything-beautiful-has -been-destroyed-palestinians-mourn-a-city-in-tatters.

10 "'Nowhere safe in Gaza': Unlawful Israeli strikes illus- trate callous disregard for Palestinian lives," Amnesty International, November 20, 2023, https://www.amnesty .org/en/latest/news/2023/11/israel-opt-nowhere-safe-in -gaza-unlawful-israeli-strikes-illustrate-callous-disregard -for-palestinian-lives/.

11 Razmig Bedirian, "The Armenian photographer who captured life in Gaza on camera: 'People had a per- sonal connection with him,'" *The National*, June 21, 2021, https://www.thenationalnews.com/arts-culture

/art/the-armenian-photographer-who-captured-life
-in-gaza-on-camera-people-had-a-personal-connection
-with-him-1.1245472; Selma Dabbagh, "Eyes on Gaza,"
London Review of Books, February 9, 2024, https:
//www.lrb.co.uk/blog/2024/february/eyes-on-gaza.

12   Sarvy Geranpayeh, "Ancient Saint Hilarion Monastery
in the Gaza Strip gains enhanced protection from
Unesco" *The Art Newspaper*, December 18, 2023,
https://www.theartnewspaper.com/2023/12/18
/ancient-saint-hilarion-monastry-in-the-gaza-strip
-gains-enhanced-protection-from-unesco.

13   "Living Archaeology in Gaza," *Forensic Architecture*,
February 23, 2022 (ongoing), https://forensic-architecture
.org/investigation/living-archaeology-in-gaza.

14   "1,000-year-old Hamam al-Sammara destroyed by
Israeli bombing in Gaza," *Middle East Eye*, December
27, 2023, https://www.middleeasteye.net/live-blog/live
-blog-update/historic-1000-year-old-hamam-al
-sammara-destroyed-israeli-bombing-gaza.

15   United Nations Office for the Coordination of
Humanitarian Affairs briefing, "Hostilities in the Gaza
Strip and Israel—reported impact, 28 January 2024."

16   "No University Left Standing in Gaza," *The Intercept*,
February 9, 2024, https://theintercept.com/2024/02/09
/deconstructed-gaza-university-education/.

17   Emanuel Fabian, "Senior IDF officer censured over
demolition of Gaza university without approval," *Times
of Israel*, March 11, 2024, https://www.timesofisrael

.com/senior-idf-officer-censured-over-demolition
-of-gaza-university-without-approval/.

18 Ahmed Eldin (@ahmedeldin), "Israeli soldier @yishai
_shalev standing afront Al-Azhar university," Instagram,
January 6, 2024, https://www.instagram.com/reel/C1v
Q1YcInsv/.

19 Rhea Nayyar, "Video of Israeli Soldiers Handling Gaza
Antiquities Raises Outrage," *Hyperallergic*, February
7, 2024, https://hyperallergic.com/868269/video-of
-israel-soldiers-handling-gaza-antiquities-raises-outrage/.

Chapter Three: Rambo in the Sterile Zone

1 Mati Wagner, "Return to Gush Katif: A determined
movement emerges to resettle Israelis in Gaza," *Times
of Israel*, December 3, 2023, https://www.timesofisrael
.com/return-to-gush-katif-determined-movement
-emerges-to-resettle-israelis-in-gaza/.

2 Judith Sudilovsky, "Resettle Gaza conference strikes
at deep debate on security and destiny," *The Jerusalem
Post*, January 29, 2024, https://www.jpost.com/israel
-hamas-war/article-784221; Isaac Chotiner, "The Extreme
Ambitions of West Bank Settlers," *The New Yorker*,
November 11, 2023, https://www.newyorker.com/news
/q-and-a/the-extreme-ambitions-of-west-bank-settlers.

3 Nir Hasson, Rachel Fink, "Netanyahu Ministers Join
Thousands of Israelis in 'Resettle Gaza' Conference
Calling for Palestinians' Transfer," *Haaretz*, January 28,
2024, https://www.haaretz.com/israel-news/2024–01
-28/ty-article/ministers-from-netanyahus-party-join

-thousands-of-israelis-at-resettle-gaza-conference
/0000018d-512f-dfdc-a5ad-db7f35e10000.

4   Joshua Leifer, "The Settler Plot to Recolonize
Gaza," *The Nation*, February 11, 2025, https://www
.thenation.com/article/world/the-settler-plot-to
-recolonize-gaza/; Shane Bauer, "The Israeli Settlers
Attacking Their Palestinian Neighbors," *The New Yorker*,
February 26, 2024, https://www.newyorker.com/magazine
/2024/03/04/israel-west-bank-settlers-attacks
-palestinians.

5   "Right-wing radio host and ex-MK says he'd shoot
journalists if he were Netanyahu," *Times of Israel*,
September 14, 2010, https://www.timesofisrael.com/right
-wing-radio-host-says-he-would-shoot-journalists
-if-he-were-netanyahu/.

6   Yinon Magal (@yinonmagal), "Demand justice for
the envelope," January 10, 2024, https://x.com/Yinon
Magal/status/1745019895991914581.

7   Petition titled "Justice for the envelope" (with contact
details for Israeli traffic cop Avidan Kalfa), Atzuma,
https://www.atzuma.co.il/tzedeklaotef; The number of
signatures did not change between January 2024 and
February 2025.

8   Mared Gwyn Jones, Shona Murray, "Artificial island
off Gaza pitched by Israeli minister in EU meeting is
'irrelevant,' Borrell says," *Euronews*, January 22, 2024,
https://www.euronews.com/my-europe/2024/01/22
/artificial-island-off-gaza-pitched-by-israeli-minister
-in-eu-meeting-is-irrelevant-borrell.

9   Ariel Kahana, "US lawmakers review plan linking Gaza refugee resettlement to American aid to Arab countries," *Israel Today*, December 1, 2023, https://www.israeltoday.co.il/read/us-lawmakers-review-plan-linking-gaza-refugee-resettlement-to-american-aid-to-arab-countries/.

10 Nir Hasson, Rachel Fink, "Netanyahu Ministers Join Thousands of Israelis in 'Resettle Gaza' Conference Calling for Palestinians' Transfer," *Haaretz*, January 28, 2024, https://www.haaretz.com/israel-news/2024-01-28/ty-article/ministers-from-netanyahus-party-join-thousands-of-israelis-at-resettle-gaza-conference/0000018d-512f-dfdc-a5ad-db7f35e10000.

11 Barak Ravid, "Israeli defense chief tells U.S. he won't allow rebuilding of settlements in Gaza," *Axios*, January 29, 2024, https://www.axios.com/2024/01/29/israel-gaza-settlements-buffer-gallant-blinken-biden.

12 "Gallant: Israel to keep military control in Gaza after war, aiming to operate there like in West Bank," *Times of Israel*, January 30, 2024, https://www.timesofisrael.com/liveblog_entry/gallant-israel-to-keep-military-control-in-gaza-after-war-aiming-to-operate-there-like-in-west-bank/.

13 "By Hook and By Crook: Israeli Settlement Policy in the West Bank," B'Tselem, July 2010; Mustafa Fetouri, "What is 'Firing Zone 918' and how Israel uses it to grab more Palestinian land," *Middle East Monitor*, October 5, 2023, https://www.middleeastmonitor.com/20231005-what-is-firing-zone-918-and-how-israel-uses-it-to-grab-more-palestinian-land/.

14   Jamie Dettmer, "Prominent settler leader pushes Netanyahu to rebuild Israeli homes in Gaza," *Politico*, November 16, 2023, https://www.politico.eu/article /prominent-settler-pushes-pm-benjamin-netanyahu -rebuild-israeli-homes-gaza/.

15   "State Business: Israel's misappropriation of land in the West Bank through settler violence," B'Tselem, November 2021.

16   Tareq Baconi, "Enforcing Apartheid in the West Bank," *New York Review of Books*, March 3, 2023.

17   "Nip Messianic Fantasies in the Bud: Jewish Settlements in Gaza Cannot Be Re-established," *Haaretz*, November 9, 2023, https://www.haaretz.com/opinion/editorial/2023 -11-09/ty-article/at-the-end-of-israels-war-we-cannot -rebuild-gush-katif-in-gaza/0000018b-b0c0-dea2 -a9bf-f0dea1ff0000.

18   "Extremist MK Ben Gvir pulls out gun during Sheikh Jarrah clash," *Times of Israel*, October 14, 2022, https: //www.timesofisrael.com/extremist-mk-ben-gvir -pulls-out-gun-during-sheikh-jarrah-clashes/; "Ben-Gvir, National Unity threaten to leave gov't over hostage deal," *The Jerusalem Post*, January 30, 2024, https: //www.jpost.com/breaking-news/article-784278.

19   Orly Noy, "The Israeli public has embraced the Smotrich doctrine," *+972 Magazine*, November 10, 2023, https: //www.972mag.com/smotrich-decisive-plan-israeli -public/.

20   Barak Ravid, "Biden issues executive order targeting Israeli settlers who attack Palestinians," *Axios*, February 1,

2024, https://www.axios.com/2024/02/01/biden-israel
-settler-violence-palestinians-executive-order.

21   Bezalel Smotrich, "Israel's Decisive Plan," *Hashiloach*,
     September 2017.

Chapter Four: Where's Daddy?

1   Amanda Taub, "Israel's Account of Attack on Aid
     Convoy Raises Wider Legal Questions, Experts Say,"
     The New York Times, April 8, 2024, https://www
     .nytimes.com/2024/04/08/world/europe/world-central
     -kitchen-strike-israel-law.html.

2   "Effective immediately, the order granted mid-ranking
     Israeli officers the authority to strike thousands of mili-
     tants and military sites that had never been a priority
     in previous wars in Gaza. Officers could now pursue
     not only the senior Hamas commanders, arms depots
     and rocket launchers that were the focus of earlier cam-
     paigns, but also the lowest-ranking fighters. In each
     strike, the order said, officers had the authority to risk
     killing up to 20 civilians.
         "The order, which has not previously been
     reported, had no precedent in Israeli military history.
     Mid-ranking officers had never been given so much
     leeway to attack so many targets, many of which had
     lower military significance, at such a high potential
     civilian cost." See Patrick Kingsley, Natan Odenheimer,
     Bilal Shbair, Ronen Bergman, John Ismay, Sheera
     Frenkel, Adam Sella, "Israel Loosened Its Rules to
     Bomb Hamas Fighters, Killing Many More Civilians,"
     The New York Times, December 26, 2024, https://www

.nytimes.com/2024/12/26/world/middleeast/israel
-hamas-gaza-bombing.html.

3   Yuval Abraham, "'Lavender': The AI machine directing Israeli's bombing spree in Gaza," *+972 Magazine*,
April 3, 2024, https://www.972mag.com/lavender
-ai-israeli-army-gaza/; "'A mass assassination factory':
Inside Israel's calculated bombing of Gaza," *+972
Magazine*, November 30, 2023, https://www.972mag
.com/mass-assassination-factory-israel-calculated
-bombing-gaza/; see also Sophia Goodfriend, "Kill
Lists," *London Review of Books*, October 10, 2024.

4   Melanie Lidman, "Amid outcry over Gaza tactics, videos of soldiers acting maliciously create new headache
for Israel," Associated Press, December 13, 2023, https:
//apnews.com/article/israel-hamas-soldiers-gaza-viral
-videos-idf-072894147302535cc9632863888e53a4;
Chantal Da Silva, "'Everybody is scared': As Gaza faces
threat of ground invasion, tensions run high in Israel,"
NBC, October 13, 2023, https://www.nbcnews.com
/news/world/everybody-scared-gaza-faces-threat
-ground-invasion-tensions-run-high-i-rcna120346.

5   Bethan McKernan, Harry Davies, "'The machine did it
coldly': Israel used AI to identify 37,000 Hamas targets,"
The Guardian, April 3, 2024, https://www.theguardian
.com/world/2024/apr/03/israel-gaza-ai-database
-hamas-airstrikes.

6   Yaniv Kubovich, "Israel Created 'Kill Zones' in
Gaza. Anyone Who Crosses into Them Is Shot,"
Haaretz, March 31, 2024, https://www.haaretz.com
/israel-news/2024–03-31/ty-article-magazine/.pre

mium/israel-created-kill-zones-in-gaza-anyone-who
-crosses-into-them-is-shot/0000018e-946c-d4de-afee
-f46da9ee0000.

7   Yaniv Kubovich, "Investigation Into Killing of Israeli
     Hostages by IDF Reveals a String of Errors and
     Flaws," *Haaretz*, December 21, 2023, https://www
     .haaretz.com/israel-news/2023–12-21/ty-article/.premium
     /investigation-into-killing-of-israeli-hostages-by
     -idf-reveals-a-string-of-errors-and-flaws/0000018c
     -890c-d60e-afdf-ed0ec51e0000.

8   Chris McGreal, "'Not a normal war:' doctors say chil-
     dren have been targeted by Israeli snipers in Gaza,"
     The Guardian, April 2, 2024, https://www.theguardian
     .com/world/2024/apr/02/gaza-palestinian-children
     -killed-idf-israel-war; Office of the United Nations
     High Commissioner for Human Rights, "UN experts
     appalled by reported human rights violations against
     Palestinian women and girls," February 19, 2024.

9   Shayan Sardarizadeh, Benedict Garman, Thomas
     Spencer, "Gaza aid convoy strike: What we know," BBC,
     April 5, 2024, https://www.bbc.co.uk/news/world
     -middle-east-68714128; Yaniv Kubovich, "IDF Drone
     Bombed World Central Kitchen Aid Convoy Three
     Times, Targeting Armed Hamas Member Who Wasn't
     There," *Haaretz*, April 2, 2024, https://www.haaretz
     .com/israel-news/2024–04-02/ty-article/.premium
     /idf-bombed-wck-aid-convoy-3-times-targeting
     -armed-hamas-member-who-wasnt-there/0000018e
     -9e75-d764-adff-9eff29360000.

10　"Open-Fire Policy," B'Tselem, November 2017; see also analysis collected by the rights group Yesh Din showing an Israeli soldier injuring a Palestinian in the West Bank has a less than 1 percent chance of ever being convicted in an Israeli court, "Law enforcement against Israeli soldiers suspected of harming Palestinians and their property—Summary of figures for 2017–2021," Yesh Din, December 21, 2022, https://www.yesh-din .org/en/law-enforcement-against-israeli-soldiers -suspected-of-harming-palestinians-and-their-property -summary-of-figures-for-2017–2021/.

11　Andrew Bernard, "White House 'outraged' over strike on aid workers as British victims named," *The Jewish Chronicle*, April 2, 2024, https://www.thejc.com/news /israel/white-house-outraged-over-strike-on-aid-workers -as-british-victims-named-tdo32da1; The original record of the April 2 press conference when Kirby spoke has been wiped from the White House website.

Chapter Five: In the Dock, Part I

1　Application of the Convention on the Prevention and Punishment of the Crime of Genocide in the Gaza Strip (South Africa v. Israel), International Court of Justice, Verbatim Record, January 12, 2024.

2　Helen Regan, Chris Lau, "Hundreds of thousands are starving in Gaza as famine arrives at 'incredible speed' UN aid chief warns," CNN, January 16, 2024, https: //edition.cnn.com/2024/01/16/middleeast/gaza-famine -starvation-un-israel-war-intl-hnk/index.html.

3   In January the housing damage estimate was 45 percent; as of February 2025 it is 90 percent. Office of the United Nations High Commissioner for Human Rights, "Destroying civilian housing and infrastructure is an international crime, warns UN expert," November 8, 2023; "Brigade 828 says 'Peace to Shujaiya': Dramatic Evidence of the Demolition of 56 Buildings in Gaza Neighbourhood," ynet, December 12, 2023; Ylenia Gostoli, Abdelhakim Abu Riash, "'We were baptised here and we will die here': Gaza's oldest church bombed," Al Jazeera, October 20, 2023, https://www.aljazeera.com/features/2023/10/20/we-were-baptised-here-and-we-will-die-here-gazas-oldest-church-bombed; "Images show major damage to Gaza's oldest mosque," BBC, December 8, 2023, https://www.bbc.co.uk/news/world-middle-east-67664853.

4   "Israel Gaza: Hostages shot by IDF put out 'SOS' sign written with leftover food," BBC, December 17th, 2023, https://www.bbc.com/news/world-middle-east-67745092.

5   "Nearly 600 attacks on healthcare in Gaza and West Bank since war began: WHO," United Nations, January 5, 2024, https://news.un.org/en/story/2024/01/1145317.

6   Application instituting proceedings and request for the indication of provisional measures (South Africa v. Israel), International Court of Justice, December 29, 2023.

7   The original publication of this article in the *New Republic* falsely attributed to Shaw the claim that

Smotrich and Ben-Gvir were "the principals of the 'war cabinet'" directing the war. Neither man was in the war cabinet at the time. This error is regretted and corrected here. I still retain absolute contempt for the stooges and suck-ups at the "Committee for Accuracy in Middle East Reporting and Analysis," even if they were right for pointing out my fault just this once.

8   Nathan Vanderklippe, "Israel is not in violation of humanitarian law, Israeli jurist says," *The Globe and Mail*, November 1, 2023, https://www.theglobeand mail.com/world/article-israel-not-in-violation-of -humanitarian-law-according-to-preeminent/.

Chapter Six: In the Dock, Part II

1   Melanie Lidman, "Amid outcry over Gaza tactics, videos of soldiers acting maliciously create new head-ache for Israel," Associated Press, December 13, 2023; Chantal Da Silva, "'Everybody is scared': As Gaza faces threat of ground invasion, tensions run high in Israel," NBC, October 13, 2023.

2   Application of the Convention on the Prevention and Punishment of the Crime of Genocide in the Gaza Strip (South Africa v. Israel), Request for the indication of provisional measures, International Court of Justice, January 26, 2024.

3   Joint press point by Roberta Metsola, EP President, Ursula von der Leyen, EC President, and Isaac Herzog, President of Israel, European Parliament, October 13, 2023, https://multimedia.europarl.europa.eu/en/video

/joint-press-point-by-roberta-metsola-ep-president
-ursula-von-der-leyen-ec-president-and-isaac-herzog
-president-of-israel_I247767.

4   U.S. Arms Sales and Human Rights: Legislative Basis and
     Frequently Asked Questions, Congressional Research
     Service, November 21, 2024.

Chapter Seven: In the Dock, Part III

1   David Gritten, "Gaza war: Where has Israel told
     Rafah displaced to go?," May 7, 2024, https://www
     .bbc.com/news/articles/c2le2njgjvlo; Kayleen Devlin,
     Maryam Ahmed, Daniele Palumbo, "Half of Gaza
     water sites damaged or destroyed, BBC satellite data
     reveals," May 9, 2024, https://www.bbc.co.uk/news
     /world-middle-east-68969239.

2   Médecins Sans Frontières (@MSF), "People in #Gaza
     tell us the number of times they've been displaced
     within the Strip before arriving in Rafah," https://x.com
     /MSF/status/1777644121382961549.

3   Neri Zilber, "Pier opens for Gaza aid as US warns of
     'imminent famine,'" *Financial Times*, May 17, 2024,
     https://www.ft.com/content/82980ad2-05b4-4ec1
     -8836-5dd86dc90984.

4   Fred Abrahams, "When White Flags Turn Red in
     Gaza," Human Rights Watch, December 18, 2023,
     https://www.hrw.org/news/2023/12/18/when-white
     -flags-turn-red-gaza.

5   Application of the Convention on the Prevention and Punishment of the Crime of Genocide in the Gaza Strip (South Africa v. Israel), Verbatim Record, International Court of Justice, May 16, 2024.

6   Application of the Convention on the Prevention and Punishment of the Crime of Genocide in the Gaza Strip (South Africa v. Israel), Urgent Request for the Modification and Indication of Provisional Measures Pursuant to Article 41 of the Statute of the International Court of Justice and Articles 75 and 76 of the Rules of the Court of the International Court of Justice, May 10, 2024.

7   Application of the Convention on the Prevention and Punishment of the Crime of Genocide in the Gaza Strip (South Africa v. Israel), Verbatim Record, International Court of Justice, May 17, 2024.

8   Dan Williams, Nidal Al-Mughrabi, "Israeli troops exit Gaza's Shifa Hospital, leaving rubble and bodies," Reuters, April 1, 2024, https://www.reuters.com/world/middle-east/israeli-troops-leave-gazas-al-shifa-hospital-after-two-week-sweep-2024-04-01/.

9   Aya Batrawy, "One man's search for his father in mass graves at Gaza's Al Shifa hospital," NPR, April 18, 2024, https://www.npr.org/2024/04/18/1245654891/one-mans-search-for-his-father-in-mass-graves-at-gazas-al-shifa-hospital.

10   Federica Marsi, "Gaza's mass graves: Is the truth being uncovered?," Al Jazeera, May 11, 2024, https://www.aljazeera.com/news/2024/5/11/gazas-mass-graves-is-the-truth-being-uncovered.

11 I. F. Stone, "What It's Like to Be in Saigon," *In a Time of Torment* (Jonathan Cape, 1968), 273.

12 John Ramming Chappell, "Key Takeaways from Biden Administration Report on Israeli Use of US Weapons," *Just Security*, May 11, 2024, https://www.justsecurity .org/95583/israel-weapons-hamas-us-report-take aways/; see also "Unlawful Use of US-Made Munitions and Violations of International Law by Israel Since January 2023," research briefing submitted by Amnesty International as part of NSM-20, April 29, 2024.

13 Rob Schmitz, "How Israel's military investigates itself in cases of possible wrongdoing," NPR, May 15, 2024, https://www.npr.org/2024/05/15/1250417719 /israel-military-idf-investigations-icc.

14 Jeremy Sharon, "Ben Gvir calls to 'encourage emigra-tion,' resettle Gaza at ultra-nationalist rally," *Times of Israel*, May 14, 2024, https://www.timesofisrael.com /ben-gvir-calls-to-encourage-emigration-resettle-gaza -at-ultra-nationalist-rally/.

15 Noa Shpigel, "Israel's Far-right Minister Smotrich Calls for 'No Half Measures' in the 'Total Annihilation' of Gaza," *Haaretz*, April 30, 2024, https://www .haaretz.com/israel-news/2024-04-30/ty-article/.premium /smotrich-calls-for-no-half-measures-in-the-total-annihilation -of-gaza/0000018f-2f4c-d9c3-abcf-7f7d25460000.

16 Aya Batrawy, Anas Baba, "A baby girl born orphaned and premature after an Israeli airstrike in Gaza has died," NPR, April 26, 2024, https://www.npr.org/2024 /04/26/1247453317/gaza-baby-girl-mother-killed -israel-airstrike.

Chapter Eight: With Haste to the Holding Cells

1   Situation in the State of Palestine: ICC Pre-Trial Chamber I rejects the State of Israel's challenges to jurisdiction and issues warrants of arrest for Benjamin Netanyahu and Yoav Gallant, International Criminal Court, November 21, 2024; These opening sentences have been returned to the strength of an earlier draft before publication.

2   Csongor Körömi, "Israel confirms death of Hamas military leader Mohammed Deif," *Politico*, August 1, 2024, https://www.politico.eu/article/israel-confirm-death-hamas-millitary-leader-mohammed-deif/.

3   Harry Davies, Robert Flummerfelt, "ICC prosecutor allegedly tried to suppress sexual misconduct claims against him," *The Guardian*, October 27, 2024, https://www.theguardian.com/law/2024/oct/27/icc-prosecutor-karim-khan-allegedly-tried-suppress-sexual-misconduct-claims; Talita Dias, "The ICC arrest warrants against Deif, Netanyahu and Gallant explained," Chatham House, November 26, 2024, https://www.chathamhouse.org/2024/05/icc-prosecutors-applications-arrest-warrants-explained.

4   Legal Consequences arising from the Policies and Practices of Israel in the Occupied Palestinian Territory, including East Jerusalem, Summary of the Advisory Opinion, International Court of Justice, July 19, 2024.

5   Zak Witus, "Sha'ban al-Dalou burned alive before the world. May his death awaken us," *The Guardian*, October 17, 2024, https://www.theguardian.com/comment

isfree/2024/oct/17/shaban-al-dalou-burned-alive
-israel-gaza

6   "Warned of Imminent Famine in Northern Gaza,
Speakers in Security Council Urge Immediate Ceasefire,
Sustained Aid," United Nations, SC/15895, November
12, 2024.

7   "How US and UK military airlifts have supported Israel's
war on Gaza," Al Jazeera, October 24, 2024, https:
//www.aljazeera.com/program/newsfeed/2024/10/24
/how-us-and-uk-military-airlifts-have-supported
-israels-war-on-gaza.

8   Taz Ali, "UK conducted more surveillance flights over
Gaza than any other country, data reveals," *The i Paper*,
October 25, 2024, https://inews.co.uk/news/world
/uk-conducted-more-surveillance-flights-over-gaza
-than-any-other-country-data-reveals-3344587.

9   Patrick Wintour, "UK government challenged over
ICC inquiry into Israel's conduct," *The Guardian*,
November 12, 2023, https://www.theguardian.com
/law/2023/nov/12/uk-government-challenged-over
-icc-inquiry-into-israels-conduct.

10 Louisa Brooke-Holland, UK arms exports to Israel,
Research Briefing, House of Commons Library, UK
Parliament, January 8, 2025.

11 PM statement on one-year anniversary of the October
7th attacks, Prime Minister's Office, 10 Downing
Street, October 6, 2024.

Chapter Nine: The Twilight of American Prestige

1   Y. L. Al-Sheikh, "Biden's Spokespeople Are the Perfect
    Vessels for His Soulless Gaza Policies," *The Nation*,
    March 13, 2024, https://www.thenation.com/article
    /politics/biden-press-secretaries-gaza-matthew-miller
    -john-kirby/.

2   "(November 22)—There will not be a Department
    Press Briefing Today," U.S. Department of State,
    November 21, 2024.

3   Gideon Rachman, "Is there such a thing as a rules-
    based international order?," *Financial Times*, April 30,
    2023, https://www.ft.com/content/664d7fa5-d575-45da
    -8129-095647c8abe7.

4   Humeyra Pamuk, Patricia Zengerle, Simon Lewis,
    "U.S. top diplomat Blinken urges all ICC members to
    comply with Putin arrest warrant," Reuters, March 22,
    2023,https://www.reuters.com/world/us-top-diplomat
    -blinken-urges-all-icc-members-comply-with-putin
    -arrest-warrant-2023–03-22/.

5   Statement from President Joe Biden on Warrants
    Issued by the International Criminal Court, The White
    House, November 21, 2024.

6   Lindsey Graham (@LindseyGrahamSC), "To President
    Biden, President Trump, and current and future mem-
    bers of Congress," November 21, 2024, https://x.com
    /LindseyGrahamSC/status/1859615266621010166.

7   "Hague Invasion Act Becomes Law," Human Rights
    Watch, August 3, 2002, https://www.hrw.org/news
    /2002/08/03/us-hague-invasion-act-becomes-law.

8 Ali Harb, "Despite 30-day Gaza aid ultimatum, US says support for Israel will proceed," Al Jazeera, November 12, 2024, https://www.aljazeera.com/news /2024/11/12/despite-thirty-day-gaza-aid-ultimatum-us -says-support-for-israel-will-proceed; Diaa Ostaz, "Northern Gaza trapped in catastrophic humanitarian situation, UN report says," ABC News, November 24, 2024, https://abcnews.go.com/International/northern -gaza-trapped-catastrophic-humanitarian-situation -report/story?id=116156231; "Humanitarian Situation Update #237," United Nations Office for the Coordination of Humanitarian Affairs, November 12, 2024.

9 Kevin Liptak, "How Joe Biden's red line on Israel went from a 'parlor game' to a murky millstone," CNN, May 30, 2024, https://edition.cnn.com/2024/05/30 /politics/joe-biden-red-line-israel/index.html.

Chapter Ten: The Intellectuals Lose Their Minds

1 Howard Jacobson, "Charging Jews with genocide is to declare them guilty of precisely what was done to them," *The Observer*, December 3, 2023, https: //www.theguardian.com/commentisfree/2023/dec/03 /charging-jews-with-genocide-declare-them-guilty -precisely-what-was-done-to-them-middle-east.

2 James Robins, "A few cheap tears," *New Humanist*, Summer 2020.

3 Simon Sebag Montefiore, "The Decolonization Narrative Is Dangerous and False," *The Atlantic*, October 27, 2023, https://www.theatlantic.com/ideas

/archive/2023/10/decolonization-narrative-dangerous
-and-false/675799/; Hadley Freeman, "We Jews aren't
even allowed posters of loved ones," *The Times*, November
5, 2023, https://www.thetimes.com/article/we-jews
-arent-even-allowed-posters-of-loved-ones-7xz8j06b7;
Zoe Strimpel, "The West remains haunted by medieval,
anti-Jewish blood libel," *The Telegraph*, November 18,
2023, https://www.telegraph.co.uk/news/2023/11/18
/west-remains-haunted-by-medieval-anti-jewish-blood
-libel/; James Robins, "Douglas Murray vs the tall trees,"
The Dreadnought, April 15, 2024, https://www.the
dreadnought.news/p/douglas-murray-vs-the-tall-trees.

4   Fyodor Dostoevsky, *The Idiot*, trans. David McDuff
(Penguin Classics, 2004), 27.

5   Howard Jacobson, "The founding of Israel wasn't a
colonial act—a refugee isn't a colonist," *New Statesman*,
November 29, 2023, https://www.newstatesman.com
/ideas/2023/11/founding-israel-palestine-anti
-semitism.

6   Letter from Comrade H. Erlich in Warsaw to Comrade
Friedrich Adler (received 24th September 1929),
Socialistische Arbeiter-Internationale (SAI) Archive,
356/22, International Institute of Social History,
Amsterdam, in Jack Jacobs, "Bundist Anti-Zionism in
Interwar Poland," *Rebels Against Zion: Studies on the
Jewish Left Anti-Zionism*, ed. August Grabski (Zydowski
Instytut Historyczny, 2011), 82–83.

7   Ibid., 85–86.

Chapter Eleven: The Annihilation Plan

1   Noa Spiegel, "At the settlement conference, the establishment of 'new Gaza' is not a mirage but a working plan," *Haaretz*, October 21, 2024, https://www.haaretz.co.il/news/politics/2024–10-21/ty-article-magazine/.premium/00000192-af02-d049-a3db-bf76397e0000; Janis Laizans, Michal Yaakov Itzhaki, "On the edge of Gaza, Israeli settlers want back in," Reuters, October 21, 2024, https://www.reuters.com/world/middle-east/edge-gaza-israeli-settlers-want-back-2024–10-21/; Jeremy Sharon, "Senior ministers call for new settlements in Gaza at ultranationalist conference," *Times of Israel*, October 21, 2024, https://www.timesofisrael.com/government-ministers-call-for-new-settlements-in-gaza-at-ultranationalist-conference/.

2   Dov Lieber, Anat Peled, "Inside the Sprawling Military Zone Israel Uses to Control Gaza From Within," *The Wall Street Journal*, December 6, 2024, https://www.wsj.com/world/middle-east/netzarim-corridor-israel-military-base-gaza-c01ec561.

3   Gus Contreras, Ari Shapiro, Tinbete Ermyas, "North Gaza is starving as humanitarian aid declines," NPR, October 18, 2024, https://www.npr.org/2024/10/18/nx-s1–5156064/north-gaza-is-starving-as-humanitarian-aid-declines.

4   Olive Enokido-Lineham, "What satellite images tell us about North Gaza as report accuses Israel of 'ethnic cleansing,'" Sky News, November 18, 2024, https://news.sky.com/story/what-satellite-images-tell-us-about-north-gaza-as-report-accuses-israel-of-ethnic-cleansing-13253674.

5   "Netanyahu's ex–defense chief Ya'alon warns Israel on path of 'ethnic cleansing' in Gaza," *Times of Israel*, November 30, 2024, https://www.timesofisrael.com /netanyahus-ex-defense-chief-yaalon-warns-israel-on -path-of-ethnic-cleansing-in-gaza/amp/.

6   Yaniv Kubovich, "Israeli Defense Officials: Gov't Pushing Aside Hostage Deal, Eyeing Gaza Annexation," *Haaretz*, October 13, 2024, https://www.haaretz.com /israel-news/2024–10-13/ty-article/.premium/israeli -defense-officials-govt-pushing-aside-hostage-deal -eyeing-gaza-annexation/00000192–8585-d988-a3ba -dde59a470000.

7   Hossam Shabat, Sharif Abdel Kouddous, "Death march from Beit Lahia," *Drop Site*, December 5, 2024, https://www.dropsitenews.com/p/death-march-from -beit-lahia.

8   "Israel attacks hospital in northern Gaza, leaving bodies lying in streets, director says," *The Guardian*, December 7, 2024, https://www.theguardian.com/world/2024/dec /07/israel-attacks-hospital-in-northern-gaza-leaving- bodies-lying-in-streets-director-says.

9   Ahmed Dremly, Ahmed Alsammak, "'What's left?,'" *The Intercept*, December 11, 2024, https://theintercept .com/2024/12/11/north-gaza-israel-generals-plan -survivors/.

10   Gabriela Pomeroy, "US calls deadly Israeli air strike 'horrifying,'" BBC, October 29, 2024, https://www .bbc.co.uk/news/articles/clydngkv3xko.

11   Ravit Hecht, "Retired Israeli General Giora Eiland Called for Starving Gaza. Does He Regret It?," *Haaretz*, September 27, 2024, https://www.haaretz.com/israel -news/2024–09-27/ty-article-magazine/.highlight /retired-israeli-general-giora-eiland-called-for-starving -gaza-does-he-regret-it/00000192–33f5-dc91-a1df -bffff4930000.

12   Giora Eiland, "In Defense of the 'Generals' Plan': Laying Siege to Israel's Enemy Isn't a War Crime," *Haaretz*, November 1, 2024, https://www.haaretz.com /opinion/2024–11-01/ty-article-opinion/.premium/in -defense-of-the-generals-plan-laying-siege-to-israels -enemy-isnt-a-war-crime/00000192-e406-d2fe-affe -e76f2f410000.

13   Yaniv Kubovich, Avi Scharf, "IDF Gearing Up to Remain in Gaza Until End of 2025, at Least. This Is What It Looks Like," *Haaretz*, November 13, 2024, https://www.haaretz.com/israel-news/security-aviation /2024–11-13/ty-article-magazine/.premium/idf -gearing-up-to-remain-in-gaza-until-end-of-2025-at -least-this-is-what-it-looks-like/00000193–2230 -d76d-a7db-637196a00000.

14   Jason Burke, "Israeli military to remain in Gaza for years, food minister says," *The Guardian*, November 29, 2024, https://www.theguardian.com/world/2024 /nov/29/israeli-military-to-remain-in-gaza-for-years -food-minister-says.

15   Younis Tirawi, "Israeli Settler Company Specializing in West Bank Outposts Now at Work in Northern

Gaza," *Drop Site*, December 2, 2024, https://www
.dropsitenews.com/p/israeli-private-construction
-company-beit-lahia-northern-gaza.

16   Prime Minister of Israel (@IsraeliPM), "I want to make
a few points absolutely clear," January 10, 2024 https:
//x.com/IsraeliPM/status/1745186120109846710.

17   "'Hopeless, Starving, and Besieged': Israel's Forced
Displacement of Palestinians in Gaza," Human Rights
Watch, November 14, 2024.

18   "Israel rejects HRW accusations of 'forcible transfer,' 'ethnic cleansing' in north Gaza," *Times of Israel*,
November 14, 2024, https://www.timesofisrael.com
/hrw-accuses-israel-of-forcible-transfer-ethnic-cleansing
-in-north-gaza-idf-denies/.

19   "Of the 1,213 women killed [in October 2023 alone],
at least 90 percent were killed in a residential building,
and 96 percent were killed in incidents where at least
one child was also killed. On average, in an incident
where a woman was killed, approximately six children
were also killed." From "Patterns of harm analysis:
Gaza, October 2023," Airwars, November 2024.

20   Jack Khoury, "'We Won't Leave': North Gaza Residents
Staying Put as Israeli Army Steps Up Pressure,"
Haaretz, October 10, 2024, https://www.haaretz
.com/israel-news/2024–10-10/ty-article/.premium/we
-wont-leave-north-gaza-residents-staying-put-as
-israeli-army-steps-up-pressure/00000192–759e-dcf6
-abd2–7fde9c780000.

Chapter Twelve: Not the End, Maybe the Beginning

1   Najib Jobain, Samy Magdy, Josef Federman, "Mediators herald Gaza ceasefire and hostage deal. Israel says final details are in flux," Associated Press, January 16, 2025, https://apnews.com/article/gaza-israel-hamas-ceasefire-334ecc4420fe3b6fce9f7a27ca886b65.

2   "Al Jazeera reporter in Gaza removes protective gear," Al Jazeera, January 16, 2025, https://www.aljazeera.com/program/newsfeed/2025/1/16/al-jazeera-reporter-in-gaza-removes-protective-gear.

3   The number of journalists killed is 169 as of mid-February 2025, "Journalist casualties in the Israel-Gaza war," Committee to Protect Journalists, February 4, 2025.

4   "What do we know about the Israel-Gaza ceasefire deal?," *Al Jazeera*, January 15, 2025, https://www.aljazeera.com/news/2025/1/15/what-do-we-know-about-the-israel-gaza-ceasefire-deal.

5   Bethan McKernan, "Netanyahu: no vote on Gaza ceasefire deal until Hamas accepts all terms," *The Guardian*, January 16, 2025, https://www.theguardian.com/world/2025/jan/16/benjamin-netanyahu-no-vote-on-gaza-ceasefire-deal-until-hamas-accepts-all-terms; "Ben Gvir says he repeatedly foiled hostage deals, urges Smotrich to help him stop this one," *Times of Israel*, January 14, 2025, https://www.timesofisrael.com/ben-gvir-says-he-repeatedly-foiled-hostage-deals-urges-smotrich-to-help-him-stop-this-one/.

6   Mehul Srivastava, Heba Saleh, Malaika Kanaaneh Tapper, Aditi Bhandari, "How Israel erased a town

of 200,000," *Financial Times*, January 14, 2025, https://www.ft.com/content/8d0f5f49-9ab1-43b0 -be1c-5a077e4e7e29.

7   Anna Noryskiewicz, "Poland clears Israel's Netanyahu to visit for Auschwitz memorial despite war crimes indictment," CBS News, January 10, 2025, https://www.cbsnews.com/news/poland-netanyahu-aus chwitz-memorial-icc-war-crimes-indictment/.

8   Pankaj Mishra, "The Shoah after Gaza," *London Review of Books*, 21 March 2024.

9   Yoel Elizur, "'When You Leave Israel and Enter Gaza, You Are God': Inside the Minds of IDF Soldiers Who Commit War Crimes," *Haaretz*, December 23, 2024, https://www.haaretz.com/2024-12-23/ty-article /.premium/when-you-enter-gaza-you-are-god-inside -the-minds-of-idf-soldiers-who-commit-war-crimes /00000193-f043-d354-a59f-ff670ac80000.

Epilogue: Genocide on Trial

1   Raz Segal, "A Textbook Case of Genocide," *Jewish Currents*, October 13, 2023, https://jewishcurrents.org /a-textbook-case-of-genocide.

2   "Public Statement: Scholars Warn of Potential Genocide in Gaza," Opinio Juris, October 18, 2023, https://opiniojuris.org/2023/10/18/public-statement -scholars-warn-of-potential-genocide-in-gaza/.

3   Ed Pilkington, "Top UN official in New York steps down citing 'genocide' of Palestinian civilians," *The*

Guardian, October 31, 2023, https://www.theguardian.com/world/2023/oct/31/un-official-resigns-israel-hamas-war-palestine-new-york.

4   "Three rights groups file ICC lawsuit against Israel over Gaza 'genocide,'" Al Jazeera, November 9, 2023, https://www.aljazeera.com/news/2023/11/9/three-rights-groups-file-icc-lawsuit-against-israel-over-gaza-genocide.

5   Convention on the Prevention and Punishment of the Crime of Genocide, Approved and proposed for signature and ratification or accession by General Assembly resolution 260 A (III), December 9, 1948.

6   Mari Cohen, "Can Genocide Studies Survive a Genocide in Gaza?" *Jewish Currents*, Fall/Winter 2024.

7   A. Dirk Moses, *The Problems of Genocide: Permanent Security and the Language of Transgression* (Cambridge University Press, 2021), vii; 27.

8   Raphael Lemkin, *Axis Rule in Occupied Europe: Laws of Occupation, Analysis of Government, Proposals for Redress* (Carnegie Endowment for Peace, 1944), 79.

9   James Loeffler, "Becoming Cleopatra: the forgotten Zionism of Raphael Lemkin," *Journal of Genocide Research* 19, no. 3, 2017, 340–360.

10   See Moses, "Genocide Studies and the Repression of the Political," in *The Problems of Genocide*, 441–476, 480.

11   When he wrote of "cultural" groups, Lemkin was generally referring to small nations such as Poland or

Czechoslovakia. When he spoke of "biological" groups, he always invariably meant Jews. One collective was "imagined," the other was "real"—bound by blood. And that "real," "biological" collective was destroyed by a different motive than the "cultural," imagined collective.

12   Philippe Sands, *East West Street: On the Origins of Genocide and Crimes Against Humanity* (Weidenfeld & Nicolson, 2016, 188.

13   Resolution of the General Assembly 95(I) of the 11th of December 1946, Affirmation of the Principles of International Law recognized by the Charter of the Nuremberg Tribunal.

14   Sands, *East West Street*, 372.

15   Moses, *Problems of Genocide*, 223–231; Anthony Conwright, "How American Racism Sabotaged the World's Fight Against Genocide," *The Nation*, January 16, 2025, https://www.thenation.com/article/politics /us-genocide-convention-history-gaza/.

16   The first footnote on page 79 of *Axis Rule* shows Lemkin considered the word "ethnocide," which reinforces the point.

17   Samuel Moyn, *Humane: How the United States Abandoned Peace and Reinvented War* (Verso, 2022), title of Chapter Four.

18   Moses, *Problems of Genocide*, 225.

19   Ibid., 224.

20 This just-so explanation is raised by Taner Akçam in his review of Moses's book for H-Diplo Roundtable XXIV-26.

21 See "Elements of Crimes," International Criminal Court, 2013.

22 William Korey, *An Epitaph for Raphaël Lemkin* (Jacob Blaustein Institute for the Advancement of Human Rights of the American Jewish Committee, 2001), 39.

23 Anton Weiss-Wendt, "When the End Justifies the Means: Raphaël Lemkin and the Shaping of a Popular Discourse on Genocide," *Genocide Studies and Prevention: An International Journal* 13, 173–188.

INDEX